EDGARDO FERNANDEZ CLIMENT

AI-Powered Cybersecurity

The Promise and Perils of Generative AI

Copyright © 2024 by Edgardo Fernandez Climent

All rights reserved. No part of this publication may be reproduced, stored or transmitted in any form or by any means, electronic, mechanical, photocopying, recording, scanning, or otherwise without written permission from the publisher. It is illegal to copy this book, post it to a website, or distribute it by any other means without permission.

Edgardo Fernandez Climent has no responsibility for the persistence or accuracy of URLs for external or third-party Internet Websites referred to in this publication and does not guarantee that any content on such Websites is, or will remain, accurate or appropriate.

Trademarks mentioned in this book are the property of their respective owners, who are not affiliated with the author. Nothing in this book should be construed as granting any license or right to use any third-party trademarks without the written permission of the third party that may own them.

First edition

This book was professionally typeset on Reedsy. Find out more at reedsy.com

Contents

Preface	viii
1. Introduction	1
1.1 The Rise of Generative AI (GenAI) and its Potential Impact on Cybersecurity	1
1.1.1 Brief history of AI in cybersecurity	2
1.1.2 The emergence of GenAI and its unique capabilities	3
1.2 Overview of the Book's Structure and Objectives	5
1.2.1 Exploring the benefits and challenges of GenAI in cybersecurity	5
1.2.2 Guiding responsible development and deployment	7
2. Fundamentals of Generative AI in Cybersecurity	9
2.1 Understanding GenAI: Definitions, Architectures, and Applications	9
2.1.1 Defining GenAI and its key characteristics	9
2.1.2 Overview of popular GenAI architectures (e.g., GANs, VAEs, Transformers)	10
2.1.3 General applications of GenAI across industries	12
2.2 How GenAI Differs from Traditional AI in Cybersecurity	13
2.2.1 Limitations of traditional AI approaches in cybersecurity	14
2.2.2 Advantages of GenAI in handling complex and evolving threats	15
2.3 Key Use Cases for GenAI in Cybersecurity	17
2.3.1 Threat intelligence generation	18
2.3.2 Adversarial Attack Simulation	19
2.3.3 Adaptive Defense Strategies	20

3. The Promise of GenAI in Cybersecurity 23
   3.1 Enhancing Threat Detection and Prevention 23
      3.1.1 Anomaly detection 24
      3.1.2 Malware analysis 27
      3.1.3 Intrusion detection 32
   3.2 Automating Incident Response and Remediation 37
      3.2.1 Generating automated playbooks for common incidents 37
      3.2.2 Adapting response strategies based on the evolving threat landscape 40
   3.3 Improving Vulnerability Management and Risk Assessment ... 43
      3.3.1 Generating attack scenarios for proactive vulnerability assessment 43
      3.3.2 Prioritizing Vulnerabilities based on Exploitability and Impact 45
   3.4 Streamlining Security Operations and Reducing Human Error 47
      3.4.1 Automating repetitive security tasks with GenAI ... 48
      3.4.2 Augmenting human decision-making with GenAI Insights 50

4. The Perils of GenAI in Cybersecurity 53
   4.1 Bias and Fairness Concerns 53
      4.1.1 Types of biases in GenAI models 54
      4.1.2 Impact of biased GenAI on cybersecurity decision-making 56
      4.1.2 Impact of biased GenAI on cybersecurity decision-making 59
   4.2 Explainability and Interpretability Challenges 65
      4.2.1 The "black box" problem in GenAI 65
      4.2.2 Importance of explainable AI in cybersecurity 71
   4.3 Accountability and Ethical Considerations 80

4.3.1 Responsibility for GenAI-based decisions in cybersecurity 80
4.3.2 Ethical guidelines for deploying GenAI in cybersecurity   87
5. Addressing the Challenges of GenAI in Cybersecurity   94
  5.1 Techniques for Mitigating Bias in GenAI Models   95
    5.1.1 Diverse and representative training data   95
    5.1.2 Fairness-aware model architectures and optimization   97
    5.1.3 Continuous monitoring and auditing for bias   99
  5.2 Approaches to Improving Explainability and Interpretability 101
    5.2.1 Developing inherently interpretable GenAI models   102
    5.2.2 Post-hoc explanations and visualizations   104
    5.2.3 Human-in-the-loop approaches for interpretability   107
  5.3 Establishing Accountability Frameworks and Ethical Guidelines   111
    5.3.1 Defining roles and responsibilities for GenAI deployment   112
    5.3.2 Developing industry standards and best practices   115
    5.3.3 Engaging with stakeholders and incorporating societal values   118
  5.4 Collaboration Between AI Researchers, Cybersecurity Experts, and Policymakers   121
    5.4.1 Interdisciplinary Research Initiatives   122
    5.4.2 Public-private partnerships for responsible GenAI development   125
    5.4.3 International cooperation and knowledge sharing   127
6. Case Studies and Real-World Applications   130
  6.1 Successful Implementations of GenAI in Cybersecurity   130
    6.1.1 Case study 1: Adaptive threat intelligence platform   130
    6.1.2 Case study 2: Automated incident response system   134
    6.1.3 Case study 3: Proactive vulnerability management with GenAI   139

6.2 Lessons Learned from GenAI Failures or Misuse in Cybersecurity ... 143
   6.2.1 Example 1: Biased threat detection leading to false positives ... 144
   6.2.2 Example 2: Lack of explainability in automated decision-making ... 145
   6.2.3 Example 3: Ethical concerns in GenAI-powered surveillance ... 147
6.3 Future Directions and Emerging Trends ... 149
   6.3.1 Integration of GenAI with other emerging technologies (e.g., blockchain, 5G) ... 150
   6.3.2 Adversarial AI and the evolving threat landscape ... 152
   6.3.3 Personalized and context-aware cybersecurity with GenAI ... 154

7. Conclusion ... 158
   7.1 Balancing the Benefits and Risks of GenAI in Cybersecurity ... 159
      7.1.1 Recap of the promise and perils discussed in the book ... 159
      7.1.2 The need for a responsible and human-centric approach ... 161
   7.2 Recommendations for Responsible Development and Deployment of GenAI ... 163
      7.2.1 Actionable steps for organizations adopting GenAI in cybersecurity ... 164
      7.2.2 Policy recommendations for regulators and decision-makers ... 166
   7.3 The Future of AI-powered Cybersecurity and its Implications for Society ... 169
      7.3.1 Potential long-term impacts on the cybersecurity industry ... 170

7.3.2 Broader societal implications and the need for ongoing dialogue	172
Appendix A. Tools	176
Threat Detection & Prevention	176
Security Operations	177
Vulnerability Management	177
Deception Technology	178
Cloud Security Tools	178
Identity and Access Management (IAM) Tools	179
Appendix B. Resources	181
Websites	181
Books	182
Podcasts	182
About the Author	184
Also by Edgardo Fernandez Climent	187

Preface

In the ever-evolving landscape of cybersecurity, where threats grow more sophisticated and numerous by the day, the advent of Generative Artificial Intelligence (GenAI) presents both a beacon of hope and a source of intrigue. As we stand at the precipice of this transformative technology, we must examine its potential to revolutionize how we protect our digital assets while carefully considering the challenges and risks of its adoption.

"AI-Powered Cybersecurity: The Promise and Perils of Generative AI" is a comprehensive exploration of the critical intersection between cutting-edge AI and the ever-evolving field of cybersecurity. This book, with its thorough examination and practical guidance, is a must-read for cybersecurity professionals, AI researchers, policymakers, and anyone interested in understanding how GenAI can be harnessed to bolster our defenses against cyber threats while also navigating the ethical, social, and technical challenges that arise from its use.

Through in-depth analysis, real-world case studies, and expert insights, this book delves into the key applications of GenAI in cybersecurity, from enhancing threat detection and prevention to automating incident response and improving vulnerability management. It explores how GenAI can help organizations stay one step ahead of cybercriminals by generating adaptive defense strategies and proactively identifying emerging threats.

However, this book is not a one-sided celebration of GenAI's potential. It also shines a critical light on the perils that come with the technology, including concerns around bias, explainability, and accountability. It examines how biased GenAI models can lead to discriminatory outcomes and false positives, how the "black box" nature of GenAI can hinder transparency and trust, and how the lack of clear accountability frameworks can raise ethical questions about the use of GenAI in cybersecurity decision-making.

This book provides a balanced and nuanced perspective, making it a valuable resource that equips readers with the knowledge and tools they need to make informed decisions about developing and deploying GenAI in their own cybersecurity practices. It offers practical guidance on mitigating bias, improving explainability, and establishing ethical guidelines while highlighting the importance of collaboration between AI researchers, cybersecurity experts, and policymakers in shaping the future of AI-powered cybersecurity.

As we navigate this uncharted territory, we must approach the integration of GenAI into cybersecurity with optimism and caution. This book is a roadmap for that journey, offering a comprehensive understanding of the promises and perils that lie ahead and empowering readers to harness the power of GenAI in a responsible, ethical, and human-centric manner.

Whether you are a seasoned cybersecurity professional, an AI researcher, or a policymaker, this book is a unique resource that will enhance your understanding of the intersection between AI and cybersecurity. Our firm belief is that **"AI-Powered Cybersecurity: The Promise and Perils of Generative AI"** will inform, educate, and inspire meaningful conversations and collaborations that will play a pivotal role in shaping the future of our digital security in the age of AI.

1. Introduction

The cybersecurity landscape has witnessed a significant shift in recent years with the rapid advancement of Artificial Intelligence (AI) technologies. As cyber threats evolve and become more sophisticated, traditional security measures often need help to keep pace. This has led to the emergence of AI-powered cybersecurity solutions, which leverage the power of machine learning and deep learning algorithms to detect, prevent, and respond to cyber threats in real time.

Among the most promising developments in this field is the rise of Generative AI (GenAI), a subset of AI that focuses on creating new, synthetic data that resembles real-world data. GenAI has the potential to revolutionize cybersecurity by enabling the creation of realistic simulations, adaptive defense strategies, and proactive threat-hunting capabilities.

1.1 The Rise of Generative AI (GenAI) and its Potential Impact on Cybersecurity

1.1.1 Brief history of AI in cybersecurity

AI has been part of the cybersecurity landscape for several decades, with early applications focusing on rule-based and expert systems. These systems relied on predefined rules and heuristics to detect and respond to known threats. However, as the volume and complexity of cyber threats increased, these traditional approaches needed help keeping up.

In the early 2000s, machine learning techniques began to gain traction in cybersecurity. Machine learning algorithms, such as support vector machines (SVMs) and decision trees, were used to classify network traffic, detect anomalies, and identify malware. These techniques enabled cybersecurity systems to learn from historical data and improve accuracy.

The advent of deep learning in the 2010s marked a significant milestone in the evolution of AI in cybersecurity. Deep learning algorithms, such as convolutional neural networks (CNNs) and recurrent neural networks (RNNs), allow for processing large volumes of unstructured data, such as network logs and malware binaries. These algorithms could automatically learn hierarchical representations of data, enabling them to detect complex patterns and anomalies previously difficult to identify.

1. INTRODUCTION

1.1.2 The emergence of GenAI and its unique capabilities

While machine learning and deep learning have significantly advanced the state of AI in cybersecurity, they primarily focus on discriminative tasks, such as classification and prediction. Generative AI, on the other hand, aims to create new data that is similar to the data it was trained on.

The emergence of GenAI can be traced back to the development of generative models, such as Generative Adversarial Networks (GANs) and Variational Autoencoders (VAEs). These models consist of two neural networks: a generator network that creates new data and a discriminator network that evaluates the authenticity of the generated data. GenAI models can learn to generate highly realistic data samples by training these networks in an adversarial manner.

In the context of cybersecurity, GenAI offers several unique capabilities:

1. **Threat simulation:** GenAI can generate realistic simulations of cyber attacks, enabling organizations to test and validate their defense mechanisms in a safe, controlled environment. By exposing their systems to a wide range of simulated threats, organizations can identify vulnerabilities and improve their resilience against real-world attacks.

2. **Adaptive defense:** GenAI models can be trained to generate adaptive defense strategies that automatically adjust to new and evolving threats. By continuously learning from the latest threat intelligence and adapting their behavior accordingly, GenAI-powered defense systems can stay one step ahead of attackers.

3. Adversarial testing: GenAI can generate adversarial examples and carefully crafted inputs to deceive machine learning models. By testing the robustness of cybersecurity systems against these adversarial examples, organizations can identify and address potential weaknesses in their AI-powered defenses.

4. Data augmentation: GenAI can generate synthetic data for training machine learning models in cybersecurity. This is particularly useful when real-world data, such as rare or emerging cyber threats, is limited and difficult to obtain.

The unique capabilities of GenAI have the potential to enhance the effectiveness of AI-powered cybersecurity solutions. By enabling the creation of realistic simulations, adaptive defense strategies, and robust adversarial testing, GenAI can help organizations stay ahead of the ever-evolving threat landscape.

However, the adoption of GenAI in cybersecurity also raises important challenges and considerations. These include concerns about the potential for bias in generated data, the need for explainability and interpretability in GenAI models, and the ethical implications of using generative AI for cybersecurity purposes.

As we explore the promise and perils of GenAI in cybersecurity throughout this book, it is important to keep these challenges in mind and work towards developing responsible, transparent, and accountable approaches to generative AI in this critical domain.

1. INTRODUCTION

1.2 Overview of the Book's Structure and Objectives

Having laid the foundation for understanding the emergence of Generative AI (GenAI) and its potential impact on cybersecurity, let us now delve into the structure and objectives of this book. **"AI-Powered Cybersecurity: The Promise and Perils of Generative AI"** is designed to comprehensively explore the benefits and challenges associated with applying GenAI in the cybersecurity domain while offering guidance for the responsible development and deployment of these cutting-edge technologies.

1.2.1 Exploring the benefits and challenges of GenAI in cybersecurity

One of the primary objectives of this book is to provide a balanced and in-depth examination of the potential benefits and challenges of leveraging GenAI in cybersecurity. As we have seen in the previous section, GenAI offers unique capabilities that can significantly enhance the effectiveness of cybersecurity solutions. From generating realistic threat simulations and adaptive defense strategies to enabling adversarial testing and data augmentation, GenAI has the potential to revolutionize the way we detect, prevent, and respond to cyber threats.

However, it is equally important to acknowledge and address the challenges and limitations of using GenAI in cybersecurity. Throughout this book, we will explore these challenges in detail, including:

1. **Bias and fairness:** GenAI models are only as unbiased as the data

they are trained on. If the training data contains inherent biases, the generated outputs may perpetuate or even amplify these biases. In cybersecurity, biased GenAI models could lead to false positives or false negatives in threat detection, potentially resulting in discriminatory outcomes or security vulnerabilities.

2. **Explainability and interpretability:** GenAI models, particularly those based on deep learning architectures, are often considered "black boxes" due to their complexity of internal workings. This lack of transparency can hinder cybersecurity professionals' ability to understand and trust the outputs of GenAI systems, making it difficult to audit and validate their decisions.

3. **Accountability and ethics:** Using GenAI in cybersecurity raises important questions about accountability and ethics. Who is responsible when a GenAI system makes a mistake or causes harm? How can we ensure that GenAI is used in a way that aligns with human values and respects individual privacy and autonomy? Addressing these ethical considerations is crucial for GenAI's responsible cybersecurity deployment.

By exploring these challenges in-depth, this book aims to provide a nuanced understanding of the risks and limitations of GenAI in cybersecurity, enabling readers to make informed decisions about adopting and implementing these technologies in their organizations.

1. INTRODUCTION

1.2.2 Guiding responsible development and deployment

Beyond exploring the benefits and challenges of GenAI in cybersecurity, this book also seeks to provide practical guidance for the responsible development and deployment of these technologies. As the use of GenAI in cybersecurity becomes more widespread, we must establish best practices and frameworks to ensure that these systems are developed and used ethically, transparently, and accountable.

Throughout the book, we will discuss various strategies and approaches for mitigating the risks and challenges associated with GenAI in cybersecurity, such as:

1. Bias mitigation techniques: We will explore techniques for identifying and mitigating bias in GenAI models, such as using diverse and representative training data, implementing fairness constraints, and regularly auditing models for potential biases.

2. Explainable AI (XAI) methods: We will discuss various approaches to making GenAI models more explainable and interpretable, such as using inherently interpretable model architectures, providing post-hoc explanations, and incorporating human-in-the-loop feedback.

3. Ethical frameworks and guidelines: We will examine existing ethical frameworks and guidelines for developing and using AI and discuss how these principles can be adapted and applied to the specific context of GenAI in cybersecurity.

4. Collaborative approaches: We will emphasize the importance of collaboration and knowledge-sharing among cybersecurity professionals, AI researchers, policymakers, and other stakeholders to ensure that diverse perspectives and expertise inform the development and deployment of GenAI in cybersecurity.

By providing this guidance, the book aims to empower readers with the knowledge and tools they need to leverage the power of GenAI in cybersecurity while minimizing the associated risks and challenges. Through theoretical foundations, practical insights, and real-world case studies, readers will understand how to develop and deploy GenAI systems in their cybersecurity practices responsibly.

Ultimately, this book aims to help shape the future of AI-powered cybersecurity in a way that maximizes the benefits of GenAI while ensuring that these technologies are used in a manner that is ethical, transparent, and aligned with the values and interests of society as a whole. By exploring the promise and perils of GenAI in cybersecurity and providing guidance for responsible development and deployment, this book aims to contribute to a more secure, resilient, and trustworthy digital future.

2. Fundamentals of Generative AI in Cybersecurity

To effectively grasp the potential of Generative AI (GenAI) in cybersecurity, it is essential first to understand the fundamental concepts, architectures, and applications of GenAI. This section will delve into the definitions, key characteristics, popular architectures, and general applications of GenAI across various industries.

2.1 Understanding GenAI: Definitions, Architectures, and Applications

2.1.1 Defining GenAI and its key characteristics

Generative AI is a subset of artificial intelligence that focuses on creating new, synthetic data that resembles real-world data. Unlike discriminative AI models, which learn to differentiate between existing data points, generative models learn the underlying probability distribution of the training data, allowing them to generate novel data points that share similar characteristics.

The key characteristics of GenAI include:

1. **Data generation:** GenAI models can generate new data points, such as images, text, or audio, that resemble the training data distribution.

2. **Unsupervised learning:** GenAI models typically learn from unlabeled data unsupervised, without the need for explicit annotations or labels.

3. **Probability distribution modeling:** GenAI models learn to approximate the probability distribution of the training data, enabling them to capture the underlying structure and patterns.

4. **Diverse outputs:** GenAI models can generate a wide range of diverse outputs by sampling from the learned probability distribution, allowing for creating novel and varied data points.

These characteristics make GenAI a powerful tool for various applications, including data augmentation, anomaly detection, and simulation.

2.1.2 Overview of popular GenAI architectures (e.g., GANs, VAEs, Transformers)

Several GenAI architectures have gained prominence in recent years, each with strengths and weaknesses. Some of the most popular GenAI architectures include:

1. **Generative Adversarial Networks (GANs):** GANs consist of two neural networks, a generator and a discriminator, that are trained in an adversarial manner. The generator learns to create synthetic

data that resembles the training data, while the discriminator learns to distinguish between real and generated data. GANs can generate highly realistic and diverse outputs through this adversarial training process.

2. Variational Autoencoders (VAEs): VAEs are generative models that learn to encode input data into a lower-dimensional latent space and then decode it back to the original data space. By sampling from the latent space, VAEs can generate new data points similar to the training data. VAEs are known for their ability to create smooth and continuous outputs.

3. Transformers: Transformers are a type of neural network architecture that has revolutionized natural language processing (NLP) tasks. While initially designed for discriminative tasks like language translation and text classification, Transformers have also been adapted for generative tasks, such as language modeling and text generation. Generative Transformer models, like GPT (Generative Pre-trained Transformer), have shown remarkable capabilities in generating coherent and contextually relevant text.

4. Flow-based models: Flow-based generative models, such as RealNVP and Glow, learn a series of invertible transformations to map the input data to a latent space and vice versa. By modeling the probability distribution in the latent space, flow-based models can generate new data points and provide exact likelihood estimates, making them useful for density estimation and anomaly detection.

Each of these GenAI architectures has strengths and weaknesses, and the choice of architecture depends on the application's specific requirements, such as the type of data, the desired output quality, and the computational resources available.

2.1.3 General applications of GenAI across industries

GenAI has found applications across a wide range of industries, showcasing its versatility and potential for innovation. Some of the general applications of GenAI include:

1. Creative industries: GenAI has been used in creative fields like art, music, and design to generate novel and unique content. For example, GANs have been used to create realistic images, videos, and 3D models, while Transformer-based models have been used to compose music and generate creative writing.

2. Healthcare and life sciences: GenAI has shown promise in various healthcare applications, such as drug discovery, medical image synthesis, and patient data generation. GenAI can help overcome privacy concerns and data scarcity issues in medical research and development by generating realistic synthetic data.

3. Finance and economics: GenAI has been applied in financial modeling, risk assessment, and fraud detection. Generative models can simulate realistic market scenarios, generate synthetic financial data for testing and validation, and detect anomalous transactions or behaviors.

4. Manufacturing and engineering: GenAI has been used in product design, simulation, and optimization. Generative models can create novel product designs, simulate complex systems and processes, and optimize manufacturing workflows.

5. Robotics and autonomous systems: GenAI has been applied in robotics to generate realistic simulations of environments and agent behaviors. By training robotic systems in these simulated environments, researchers can accelerate the development and testing of autonomous systems.

These are just a few examples of the diverse applications of GenAI across industries. As the field continues to evolve, we can expect to see even more innovative use cases emerge, leveraging the power of GenAI to solve complex problems and drive progress.

GenAI offers unique cybersecurity opportunities to enhance threat detection, improve defense strategies, and create more resilient systems. By understanding the fundamental concepts, architectures, and applications of GenAI, cybersecurity professionals can better harness its potential to stay ahead of the ever-evolving threat landscape. In the following sections, we will explore how GenAI can be applied specifically to cybersecurity tasks and the challenges and considerations of its adoption in this critical domain.

2.2 How GenAI Differs from Traditional AI in Cybersecurity

In cybersecurity, traditional AI approaches have played a significant role in detecting and mitigating threats. However, as the complexity and sophistication of cyber threats continue to grow, these conventional methods face certain limitations. In this section, we will explore the limitations of traditional AI approaches in cybersecurity and highlight the advantages of GenAI in handling complex and evolving threats.

2.2.1 Limitations of traditional AI approaches in cybersecurity

Traditional AI approaches in cybersecurity, such as rule-based systems, machine learning algorithms (e.g., support vector machines, decision trees), and shallow neural networks, have effectively addressed known threats and patterns. However, these approaches have several limitations when it comes to dealing with the ever-evolving cybersecurity landscape:

1. Reliance on labeled data: Traditional AI methods heavily rely on labeled data for training. In cybersecurity, labeled data often represents known threats or attacks. This reliance on labeled data limits the ability of these models to detect novel or previously unseen threats, as they can only learn from the examples they have been trained on.

2. Difficulty handling evolving threats: Cybercriminals constantly adapt their tactics, techniques, and procedures (TTPs) to evade detection and exploit new vulnerabilities. Once trained, traditional AI models may struggle to keep pace with these evolving threats, requiring manual updates and retraining to incorporate new threat intelligence.

3. Limited context awareness: Traditional AI approaches often focus on isolated events or indicators of compromise (IoCs) without considering the broader context in which they occur. This narrow focus can lead to false positives or false negatives, as the models may need help understanding the relationships and dependencies between different entities and events in a network.

4. Scalability and performance issues: As the volume and velocity of cybersecurity data continue to grow, traditional AI models may face scalability and performance challenges. Processing large amounts of high-dimensional data in real-time can be computationally expensive, leading to threat detection and response delays.

5. Lack of explainability: Many traditional AI models, particularly those based on complex algorithms or deep neural networks, lack explainability. Their decision-making process is often opaque, making it difficult for cybersecurity analysts to understand and trust their outputs.

These limitations highlight the need for more advanced and adaptive AI approaches in cybersecurity, which is where GenAI comes into play.

2.2.2 Advantages of GenAI in handling complex and evolving threats

GenAI offers several advantages over traditional AI approaches in addressing the challenges posed by complex and evolving cyber threats:

1. Unsupervised learning and anomaly detection: GenAI models can learn from unlabeled data in an unsupervised manner, allowing them to discover patterns and anomalies that may not have been previously known or captured in labeled datasets. This capability is particularly valuable in detecting novel or zero-day threats that evade traditional signature-based detection methods.

2. Adaptive threat modeling: GenAI models can generate realistic simulations of evolving threat scenarios, enabling cybersecurity teams to assess their defenses against potential future attacks proactively. Organizations can adapt their defense strategies to stay ahead of the ever-changing threat landscape by continuously updating these generative models with the latest threat intelligence.

3. Contextual understanding: GenAI models can be designed to capture the complex relationships and dependencies between different entities and events in a network. By learning the normal behavior patterns of users, devices, and applications, GenAI models can identify anomalous activities that deviate from these patterns, even if they have not been explicitly labeled malicious.

4. Scalability and efficiency: GenAI models can be optimized for scalability and efficiency, leveraging techniques like transfer learning, few-shot learning, and meta-learning to adapt quickly to new tasks and domains. This adaptability allows GenAI models to process large volumes of cybersecurity data more efficiently, enabling real-time threat detection and response.

5. Improved explainability: Recent advancements in explainable AI (XAI) techniques have enabled the development of GenAI models that provide more transparent and interpretable outputs. By incorporating XAI methods, such as attention mechanisms, saliency maps, and rule extraction, GenAI models can offer insights into their decision-making process, enhancing the trust and adoption of these models in cybersecurity applications.

6. Adversarial robustness: GenAI models can be trained using adversarial techniques to improve their resilience against adversarial attacks. By exposing the models to carefully crafted adversarial examples during training, GenAI models can learn to recognize and defend against deception or manipulation attempts, enhancing their robustness in real-world deployment.

These advantages demonstrate the potential of GenAI in addressing the limitations of traditional AI approaches and providing more effective, adaptive, and resilient solutions for cybersecurity challenges. As GenAI continues to evolve and mature, we can expect to see even more innovative applications and techniques emerge, further strengthening the defense against complex and evolving cyber threats.

However, it is important to note that GenAI is not a silver bullet solution for all cybersecurity problems. The adoption of GenAI in cybersecurity also comes with challenges and considerations, such as data privacy, model bias, and ethical concerns, which we will discuss in later sections of this book. Nonetheless, by understanding the unique capabilities and advantages of GenAI, cybersecurity professionals can make informed decisions about incorporating these technologies into their security strategies and workflows, ultimately enhancing their ability to protect against the ever-evolving threat landscape.

2.3 Key Use Cases for GenAI in Cybersecurity

Now that we have explored the advantages of GenAI over traditional AI approaches in cybersecurity let's delve into some of the key cases where GenAI can be applied to enhance an organization's security posture. This section will discuss three critical areas: threat intelligence generation, adversarial attack simulation, and adaptive defense strategies.

2.3.1 Threat intelligence generation

Threat intelligence is vital in proactive cybersecurity, informing organizations about the latest threats, vulnerabilities, and attack vectors. GenAI can significantly enhance threat intelligence generation by:

1. **Automated data collection and synthesis:** GenAI models can be trained to automatically collect and synthesize threat data from various sources, such as dark web forums, hacker communities, and security blogs. By learning these sources' linguistic patterns and context, GenAI models can identify and extract relevant threat information, saving time and effort for human analysts.

2. **Generating realistic threat scenarios:** GenAI models, particularly those based on Transformers or language models, can generate realistic threat scenarios by learning from historical attack patterns and tactics. These generated scenarios can help cybersecurity teams anticipate potential attack vectors and develop appropriate defense strategies.

3. **Enhancing indicator of compromise (IoC) generation:** GenAI models can generate high-quality IoCs, such as malicious IP addresses, domain names, or file hashes, by learning from known malicious samples. These generated IoCs can be used to proactively blacklist or monitor suspicious entities, improving threat detection and prevention capabilities.

4. **Identifying emerging threats:** GenAI models can be trained to identify emerging threats by analyzing large volumes of unstructured data, such as social media posts, news articles, and research papers. By detecting subtle patterns and anomalies in this data, GenAI models can

provide early warnings about new attack techniques, vulnerabilities, or threat actors before they become widespread.

By leveraging GenAI for threat intelligence generation, organizations can gain a more comprehensive and timely understanding of the threat landscape, enabling them to make informed decisions and prioritize their security efforts effectively.

2.3.2 Adversarial Attack Simulation

Adversarial attack simulation is another key use case for GenAI in cybersecurity. By generating realistic attack scenarios and testing an organization's defenses against them, GenAI can help identify vulnerabilities and improve the overall security posture. Some applications of GenAI in adversarial attack simulation include:

1. Generating adversarial examples: GenAI models like GANs can generate examples to fool or deceive machine learning-based security systems. By training defense models against these adversarial examples, organizations can improve the robustness and resilience of their AI-powered security solutions.

2. Simulating realistic attack paths: GenAI models can simulate realistic attack paths by generating sequences of actions that an attacker might take to compromise a system. These simulations can help identify potential entry points, lateral movement paths, and critical assets that attackers may target.

3. Testing incident response plans: GenAI can generate realistic attack scenarios to test an organization's incident response plans and procedures. Organizations can assess the effectiveness of their incident response strategies by simulating various attack scenarios, such as data breaches, ransomware attacks, or denial-of-service (DoS) attacks.

4. Continuous security validation: GenAI models can be integrated into continuous security validation processes, which constantly generate new attack scenarios to test the organization's defenses. This ongoing validation helps ensure that security controls remain effective against evolving threats and can quickly identify weaknesses or misconfigurations.

By leveraging GenAI for adversarial attack simulation, organizations can proactively assess and strengthen their security posture, reducing the risk of successful attacks and minimizing the potential impact of security incidents.

2.3.3 Adaptive Defense Strategies

GenAI can also be crucial in developing and implementing adaptive defense strategies that dynamically adjust to changing threat landscapes. Some applications of GenAI in adaptive defense include:

1. Anomaly detection: GenAI models, such as autoencoders or GANs, can be trained on normal system behavior and network traffic patterns. These models can identify anomalies or deviations indicating potential threats or attacks by learning the expected behavior. GenAI models can adapt and update their understanding of what constitutes anomalous behavior as new normal patterns emerge.

2. **Dynamic policy enforcement:** GenAI models can be used to develop dynamic security policies that adapt to changing risk levels or threat contexts. For example, a GenAI model can learn to adjust access controls, network segmentation rules, or authentication requirements based on factors like user behavior, device posture, or threat intelligence inputs.

3. **Automated threat hunting:** GenAI can be applied to automate threat-hunting processes by continuously analyzing large volumes of security data, such as log files, network traffic, or endpoint telemetry. By learning to identify patterns and correlations indicative of malicious activity, GenAI models can surface potential threats for further investigation by human analysts, adapting to new attack techniques as they emerge.

4. **Predictive maintenance and patch prioritization:** GenAI models can be trained to predict potential system failures or vulnerabilities using historical data and patterns. By identifying high-risk assets or configurations, these models can help prioritize maintenance activities, such as patching or upgrading systems, to mitigate potential security risks proactively.

5. **Adaptive deception techniques:** GenAI can be leveraged to create adaptive deception techniques, such as honeypots or decoy systems, that can dynamically adjust their behavior to attract and deceive potential attackers. By learning from attacker behavior and adapting the deception strategy accordingly, GenAI-powered deception can provide valuable threat intelligence and divert attackers away from critical assets.

By incorporating GenAI into adaptive defense strategies, organizations can create more dynamic, flexible, and resilient security postures that can effectively respond to the ever-evolving threat landscape. However, it is essential to consider the potential challenges and limitations of GenAI in adaptive defense, such as the need for continuous monitoring, the risk of model drift or bias, and the importance of human oversight and intervention.

In conclusion, the key use cases of GenAI in cybersecurity - threat intelligence generation, adversarial attack simulation, and adaptive defense strategies - demonstrate this technology's significant potential to revolutionize how organizations protect their assets and respond to cyber threats. By leveraging the unique capabilities of GenAI, cybersecurity professionals can gain a more proactive, adaptive, and intelligent approach to security, ultimately enhancing their ability to safeguard critical systems and data in an increasingly complex and dynamic threat landscape.

3. The Promise of GenAI in Cybersecurity

As we have explored the key use cases of GenAI in cybersecurity, it is clear that this technology holds immense promise for revolutionizing how organizations detect, prevent, and respond to cyber threats. In this section, we will dive deeper into one of the most significant areas where GenAI can make a difference: enhancing threat detection and prevention. Specifically, we will focus on anomaly detection and how GenAI can enable unsupervised learning to identify novel threats and adaptive anomaly detection.

3.1 Enhancing Threat Detection and Prevention

Effective threat detection and prevention are critical components of any robust cybersecurity strategy. As cyber threats evolve and become more sophisticated, traditional rule-based and signature-based detection methods often need help to keep pace. GenAI can play a transformative role by enabling more advanced and adaptive approaches to anomaly detection.

3.1.1 Anomaly detection

Anomaly detection is the process of identifying unusual or unexpected patterns in data that may indicate the presence of a threat or attack. In cybersecurity, anomalies can take many forms, such as unusual network traffic, suspicious user behavior, or atypical system activity. By detecting these anomalies early, organizations can quickly investigate and respond to potential threats before they escalate into full-blown security incidents.

3.1.1.1 Unsupervised learning for identifying novel threats

One of the key advantages of GenAI in anomaly detection is its ability to leverage unsupervised learning techniques to identify novel and previously unknown threats. Unsupervised learning allows GenAI models to learn from unlabeled data without explicit guidance or predefined rules. This is particularly valuable in cybersecurity, where the threat landscape constantly evolves, and new attack techniques and vectors emerge regularly.

GenAI models, such as autoencoders or generative adversarial networks (GANs), can be trained on large volumes of normal system behavior and network traffic data. By learning this data's expected patterns and characteristics, these models can develop a deep understanding of what constitutes "normal" behavior. GenAI models can identify deviations or anomalies that do not conform to the learned normal patterns when presented with new, unseen data.

For example, a GAN-based anomaly detection system can be trained on historical network traffic data, learning to generate realistic samples

3. THE PROMISE OF GENAI IN CYBERSECURITY

that mimic normal traffic. When deployed in a live environment, the system can compare incoming traffic to the generated samples, flagging any traffic that deviates from the expected patterns as potential anomalies. This approach allows the system to detect novel threats that may not match known signatures or rules, providing an additional layer of protection against evolving attack techniques.

3.1.1.2 Adaptive Anomaly Detection using GenAI

Another key benefit of GenAI in anomaly detection is its ability to adapt to changing environments and evolving threats. Traditional anomaly detection methods rely on static statistical models or predefined thresholds, which can become outdated or ineffective as system behavior and threat landscapes change. GenAI, on the other hand, can continuously learn and adapt to new patterns and anomalies, ensuring that the detection system remains effective and relevant.

One approach to adaptive anomaly detection using GenAI is online learning or incremental learning techniques. In this approach, the GenAI model is initially trained on a baseline dataset of normal behavior. As new data arrives in real time, the model can incrementally update its understanding of normal patterns, incorporating any new variations or changes. This allows the model to adapt to gradual shifts in system behavior or network traffic, reducing false positives and ensuring that the detection system remains sensitive to true anomalies.

Another approach is to leverage reinforcement learning, where the GenAI model learns to optimize its detection strategy based on feedback from the environment. In this case, the model can be rewarded for correctly identifying anomalies and penalized for false positives or false negatives. Over time, the model learns to adapt its detection thresholds and decision boundaries to maximize its performance, continuously improving its ability to detect and prioritize true threats.

Adaptive anomaly detection using GenAI can also incorporate external context and threat intelligence to enhance its effectiveness further. For example, the model can be trained to consider factors such as the criticality of assets, the risk level of users or devices, or the current threat landscape when making detection decisions. By integrating this contextual information, the GenAI-powered anomaly detection system can provide more accurate and risk-prioritized alerts, enabling security teams to focus on the most significant threats.

However, it is important to recognize that adaptive anomaly detection using GenAI is not without challenges. One key consideration is continuous monitoring and validation of the model's performance. As the model adapts to new patterns and anomalies, there is a risk of model drift or degradation over time. Regular testing, evaluation, and recalibration of the model are necessary to ensure that it remains effective and aligned with the organization's security objectives.

Another challenge is the potential for adversarial attacks targeting the GenAI-based anomaly detection system. Attackers may attempt to manipulate or poison the training data or craft adversarial examples that can evade detection. To mitigate these risks, it is crucial to implement robust security measures around the GenAI model, such as input validation, data integrity checks, and adversarial training techniques.

Despite these challenges, the promise of GenAI in enhancing threat detection and prevention through adaptive anomaly detection is significant. By leveraging the power of unsupervised learning and continuous

3. THE PROMISE OF GENAI IN CYBERSECURITY

adaptation, GenAI-powered anomaly detection systems can provide organizations with a more proactive, dynamic, and effective approach to identifying and mitigating evolving cyber threats. As the field of GenAI continues to advance, we expect to see even more sophisticated and robust anomaly detection techniques emerge, further strengthening the frontline defense against the ever-changing threat landscape.

3.1.2 Malware analysis

Malware analysis is critical to cybersecurity, as it involves examining and understanding malicious software's behavior, characteristics, and impact. Traditional malware analysis techniques rely on manual reverse engineering or signature-based detection, which can be time-consuming and ineffective against novel or obfuscated malware. GenAI has the potential to revolutionize malware analysis by enabling the generation of diverse malware samples for training detection models and facilitating the identification of malware families and variants.

3.1.2.1 Generating diverse malware samples for training detection models

One key challenge in developing effective malware detection models is the availability of diverse and representative malware samples for training. Malware authors often employ various obfuscation and evasion techniques, such as encryption, polymorphism, or metamorphism, to make their malware harder to detect and analyze. This results in various malware samples that may exhibit different behaviors and characteristics, making it difficult to build comprehensive detection models.

GenAI can address this challenge by generating synthetic malware samples that capture the diversity and complexity of real-world malware. GenAI models, such as generative adversarial networks (GANs) or variational autoencoders (VAEs), can learn the underlying patterns and features that characterize malicious code by training on a large corpus of known malware samples. These models can then generate new, unseen malware samples that exhibit behaviors and characteristics similar to real malware but with unique variations and modifications.

For example, a GAN-based malware generation model can be trained on a dataset of malware binaries, learning to generate realistic malware samples that mimic the functionality and structure of the original samples. The generator network learns to produce malware samples that can evade detection by the discriminator network, which is trained to distinguish between real and generated malware. Through this adversarial training process, the generator network can create increasingly sophisticated and diverse malware samples that can be used to train and test malware detection models.

The generated malware samples can augment existing malware datasets, providing a rich and diverse set of training examples for building more robust and generalizable detection models. GenAI-powered malware generation can help improve the models' ability to detect novel and evolving malware threats in real-world scenarios by exposing the detection models to a wide range of malware variants and behaviors during training.

However, it is important to note that the generated malware samples should be carefully controlled and contained within secure testing environments to prevent any unintended consequences or misuse. Proper safeguards and ethical considerations must be in place to ensure that the generated malware is used solely to improve malware detection and analysis capabilities.

3.1.2.2 Identifying malware families and variants

Another promising application of GenAI in malware analysis is the identification of malware families and variants. Malware families are groups of malware samples that share common code, functionality, or behavior, often created by the same malware authors or derived from the same codebase. Identifying malware families is crucial for understanding malware authors' tactics, techniques, and procedures (TTPs) and developing targeted defense strategies and attribution efforts.

GenAI can help identify malware families and variants by learning the underlying patterns and relationships among malware samples. GenAI models can learn to recognize the shared features and characteristics that define different malware families by training on a large corpus of labeled malware samples. These models can then classify new, unknown malware samples into their respective families or variants based on their similarity to known samples.

One approach to malware family identification using GenAI is through deep learning techniques, such as convolutional neural networks (CNNs) or recurrent neural networks (RNNs). These models can be trained on various features extracted from malware samples, such as binary code, API calls, or control flow graphs. By learning the hierarchical and sequential patterns in these features, deep learning models can capture the complex relationships and similarities among malware samples belonging to the same family.

For example, a CNN-based malware family classification model can be trained on visual representations of malware binaries, such as byteplot or grayscale images. The CNN learns to recognize the visual patterns and textures characteristic of different malware families, enabling it to classify new malware samples based on their visual similarity to known family samples. This approach can be particularly effective in identifying malware variants that employ obfuscation or encryption techniques, as the visual patterns may remain relatively consistent despite the modifications to the underlying code.

Another approach is to use graph neural networks (GNNs) to model the relationships and dependencies among malware samples based on their code structure or behavior. GNNs can learn to embed malware samples into a low-dimensional vector space, where samples of the same family are clustered based on their graph similarity. This allows for identifying malware families and variants based on their structural and behavioral commonalities, even in minor code modifications or obfuscations.

GenAI-powered malware family identification can provide several benefits for malware analysis and defense. By automatically grouping malware samples into families and variants, security analysts can prioritize their analysis efforts and focus on the most significant or prevalent threats. This can help accelerate the development of targeted defense strategies tailored to specific malware families, such as signature generation or behavioral detection rules.

Moreover, identifying malware families can aid in attributing malware campaigns and tracking malware authors' activities. GenAI can help security researchers build a more comprehensive understanding of the malware ecosystem and the actors behind it by uncovering the relationships and evolutionary paths among malware samples. This

3. THE PROMISE OF GENAI IN CYBERSECURITY

knowledge can inform threat intelligence efforts and support proactive defense measures, such as threat hunting or takedown operations.

However, there are also challenges and considerations associated with GenAI-based malware family identification. One challenge is the need for large and diverse malware datasets to train the models. Collecting and labeling a sufficient number of representative malware samples can be time-consuming and resource-intensive, requiring collaboration among security researchers and organizations.

Another challenge is the potential for malware authors to employ adversarial techniques to evade or deceive malware family identification models. Malware authors may deliberately introduce noise or variations in their malware samples to make them harder to classify or group together. To mitigate this risk, it is important to incorporate adversarial training techniques and regularly update the models with new and diverse malware samples to maintain their robustness and effectiveness.

Despite these challenges, the promise of GenAI in malware analysis, particularly in generating diverse malware samples and identifying malware families and variants, is significant. By leveraging the power of deep learning and generative models, GenAI can enable more efficient and effective malware analysis workflows, empowering security researchers and analysts to stay ahead of the ever-evolving malware landscape. As GenAI techniques continue to advance, we can expect to see even more sophisticated and accurate malware analysis capabilities emerge, strengthening our defense against the growing threat of malicious software.

3.1.3 Intrusion detection

Intrusion detection is a critical component of cybersecurity that focuses on identifying unauthorized access, misuse, or malicious activities within a computer system or network. Intrusion Detection Systems (IDS) are designed to monitor network traffic, system logs, and user activities to detect potential security breaches or policy violations. However, traditional IDS often need help keeping pace with modern cyber threats' evolving and sophisticated nature, such as Advanced Persistent Threats (APTs). GenAI has the potential to revolutionize intrusion detection by generating realistic network traffic for IDS training and enabling the detection of APTs.

3.1.3.1 Generating realistic network traffic for IDS training

One key challenge in developing effective intrusion detection models is the availability of representative and diverse network traffic data for training. IDS models must be trained on a wide range of normal and malicious network activities to distinguish between benign and anomalous behavior accurately. However, collecting and labeling real-world network traffic data can be time-consuming, expensive, and often limited regarding the diversity and coverage of different attack scenarios.

GenAI can address this challenge by generating synthetic network traffic data that mimics the characteristics and patterns of real-world traffic. By training on a large corpus of historical network traffic data, GenAI models, such as Generative Adversarial Networks (GANs) or Variational Autoencoders (VAEs), can learn the underlying distributions and dependencies of different traffic features, such as packet sizes,

3. THE PROMISE OF GENAI IN CYBERSECURITY

inter-arrival times, and protocol usage.

For example, a GAN-based network traffic generation model can consist of two neural networks: a generator network that produces realistic traffic samples and a discriminator network that learns to distinguish between real and generated traffic. Through an adversarial training process, the generator network learns to create increasingly realistic traffic samples that can fool the discriminator network. The resulting generated traffic can capture the diversity and complexity of real-world network activities, including both normal and malicious behaviors.

The generated network traffic can augment existing IDS training datasets, providing a rich and diverse set of examples for building more robust and generalizable detection models. By exposing the IDS models to a wide range of synthetic traffic scenarios, including novel and evolving attack patterns, GenAI-powered traffic generation can help improve the models' ability to detect previously unseen intrusions and adapt to changing threat landscapes.

Moreover, GenAI-based traffic generation can enable the creation of customized and targeted training datasets for specific network environments or attack scenarios. For instance, security researchers can use GenAI to generate traffic samples that mimic the behavior of specific APTs or exploit particular network vulnerabilities, allowing for the development of specialized IDS models tailored to detect those specific threats.

However, it is important to ensure that the generated traffic is properly labeled and validated to maintain the integrity and reliability of the IDS training process. The generated traffic should be carefully reviewed and filtered to remove unrealistic or inconsistent samples that may introduce noise or bias into the models. Additionally, the generated traffic should be combined with real-world traffic data to ensure that the IDS models are exposed to a balanced and representative mix of normal and malicious activities.

3.1.3.2 Detecting Advanced Persistent Threats (APTs)

Advanced Persistent Threats (APTs) are highly sophisticated and targeted cyber attacks designed to evade traditional security measures and maintain a long-term presence within a network. APTs are typically carried out by well-resourced and motivated adversaries, such as nation-state actors or organized crime groups, who employ a combination of social engineering, zero-day exploits, and custom malware to infiltrate and compromise target systems.

Detecting APTs is a significant challenge for intrusion detection systems due to their stealthy and persistent nature. APTs often involve multiple stages of the attack lifecycle, including initial compromise, lateral movement, data exfiltration, and long-term persistence. Each stage may employ different tactics and techniques, making it difficult to detect attacks using traditional signature-based or rule-based approaches.

GenAI can enhance the detection of APTs by learning the complex patterns and behaviors associated with these advanced threats. By training on a large corpus of APT-related data, such as network logs, system events, and threat intelligence reports, GenAI models can learn to recognize the subtle indicators and anomalies characteristic of APT activities.

One approach to APT detection using GenAI is to use sequence learning

3. THE PROMISE OF GENAI IN CYBERSECURITY

techniques, such as Recurrent Neural Networks (RNNs) or Long-Short-Term Memory (LSTM) networks. These models can learn to capture the temporal dependencies and long-range correlations among different events and activities within a network. By modeling the sequential patterns of APT behaviors, such as the order and timing of network connections, file access, and command execution, sequence learning models can detect the multi-stage and persistent nature of APT attacks.

For example, an LSTM-based APT detection model can be trained on a sequence of network flow records, system logs, and user activities over an extended period. The model learns to remember and correlate the relevant information across different time steps, allowing it to detect the subtle patterns and anomalies that may indicate an ongoing APT attack. By considering the historical context and the evolving behavior of the attack, the model can provide early warning and actionable insights for security analysts to investigate and mitigate the threat.

Another approach is to use graph neural networks (GNNs) to model the complex relationships and dependencies among different entities and activities within a network. GNNs can learn to represent the network topology, user interactions, and data flows as a graph, where nodes represent entities (e.g., devices, users, files) and edges represent relationships or interactions. By learning the structural and temporal patterns within the graph, GNNs can detect anomalous subgraphs or motifs indicative of APT activities, such as lateral movement or data exfiltration.

GenAI-powered APT detection can provide several benefits for intrusion detection and threat hunting. GenAI models can reduce reliance on analysis and signature development by automatically learning manual three's complex and evolving APT behavior patterns. This can help security teams quickly identify and respond to APT incidents, minimizing the attack's dwell time and potential impact.

Moreover, GenAI can enable the detection of previously unknown or zero-day APT attacks by learning the generalized patterns and anomalies associated with these threats. GenAI models can provide a proactive and adaptive defense against the ever-evolving APT landscape by continuously adapting to new attack techniques and behaviors.

However, there are also challenges and considerations associated with GenAI-based APT detection. One challenge is the need for large and diverse datasets that capture the full spectrum of APT activities and behaviors. Collecting and labeling such datasets can be difficult and time-consuming, requiring collaboration among multiple organizations and threat intelligence providers.

Another challenge is the potential for adversarial attacks and evasion techniques designed to deceive or bypass GenAI-based detection models. APT actors may employ adversarial machine learning techniques to generate malicious samples that can evade detection or manipulate the training data to degrade the model's performance. To mitigate these risks, it is important to incorporate adversarial training and robustness measures into the GenAI models and regularly update and validate them against new and emerging APT threats.

Despite these challenges, the promise of GenAI in intrusion detection, particularly in generating realistic network traffic for IDS training and detecting Advanced Persistent Threats, is significant. By leveraging the power of deep learning and generative models, GenAI can enable more effective and adaptive intrusion detection capabilities, empowering organizations to defend against the most sophisticated and persistent cyber threats. As GenAI techniques advance, we can expect to see even more innovative and robust approaches to intrusion detection, strengthening the frontline defense against the ever-evolving threat landscape.

3.2 Automating Incident Response and Remediation

Incident response and remediation are critical processes in cybersecurity that involve detecting, analyzing, and mitigating security incidents to minimize their impact and prevent future occurrences. However, traditional incident response approaches often rely on manual and reactive measures, which can be time-consuming, error-prone, and ineffective against cyber threats' growing volume and complexity. GenAI can revolutionize incident response and remediation by automating common incident handling tasks and adapting response strategies based on the evolving threat landscape.

3.2.1 Generating automated playbooks for common incidents

One key challenge in incident response is the need for quick and consistent actions to contain and eradicate security incidents. Incident response teams often have to follow predefined playbooks or runbooks that outline the step-by-step procedures for handling specific incidents, such as malware infections, data breaches, or network intrusions. However, creating and maintaining these playbooks can be labor-intensive and time-consuming, requiring significant manual effort and domain expertise.

GenAI can automate the generation of incident response playbooks by learning from historical incident data and security best practices. By training on a large corpus of past incident reports, investigation logs, and remediation actions, GenAI models, such as language or sequence-to-sequence models, can learn the common patterns and workflows associated with different incidents.

For example, a GenAI-based playbook generation model can be trained on a dataset of historical phishing incidents, learning the typical steps in detecting, analyzing, and mitigating phishing attacks. The model can learn to generate a structured playbook that includes tasks such as:

1. Identifying the phishing email and its recipients.
2. Analyzing the email content, attachments, and links for malicious indicators.
3. Quarantining or deleting the email from user inboxes.
4. Blocking the malicious domains or IP addresses associated with the phishing campaign.
5. Resetting passwords for compromised user accounts.
6. Conducting user awareness training and education.

The generated playbook can be further customized and refined based on the organization's specific requirements and policies, ensuring that the incident response actions align with the organization's risk management and compliance frameworks.

GenAI can help organizations standardize and streamline their incident-handling processes by automating the generation of incident response playbooks. This can reduce the time and effort required to create and update playbooks manually, enabling faster and more consistent incident response actions and minimizing the potential impact and duration of security incidents.

Moreover, GenAI-generated playbooks can be dynamically adapted and updated based on new incident data and emerging threat intelligence. As new types of incidents or attack techniques are encountered, the GenAI models can learn from these experiences and generate updated playbooks incorporating the latest best practices and mitigation strategies. This can help organizations maintain a continuous and proactive incident response posture, keeping pace with the evolving threat landscape.

However, it is important to note that human experts should review and validate the generated playbooks to ensure their accuracy, relevance, and compliance with organizational policies and regulations. The playbooks should be treated as decision support tools rather than fully autonomous solutions, allowing human analysts to exercise their judgment and expertise in handling complex or novel incident scenarios.

3.2.2 Adapting response strategies based on the evolving threat landscape

Another key challenge in incident response is adapting and evolving response strategies based on the changing nature of cyber threats. As new attack techniques, vulnerabilities, and threat actors emerge, organizations must continuously update and refine their incident response approaches to effectively detect, investigate, and mitigate these evolving threats.

GenAI can enable the adaptation of incident response strategies by learning from real-time threat intelligence and security event data. By ingesting and analyzing large volumes of structured and unstructured data from various sources, such as threat intelligence feeds, security blogs, social media, and dark web forums, GenAI models can learn to identify emerging trends, patterns, and indicators of new or evolving threats.

For example, a GenAI-based threat intelligence model can be trained on a continuous stream of security event data, such as network logs, endpoint telemetry, and intrusion detection alerts. The model can learn to recognize the changing tactics, techniques, and procedures (TTPs) employed by different threat actors, such as using new exploit kits, phishing templates, or command-and-control infrastructure.

The GenAI model can dynamically generate and recommend adaptations to the organization's incident response strategies based on the insights gained from this real-time threat intelligence. For instance, if the model detects a new type of ransomware campaign targeting a specific industry sector, it can generate recommendations such as:

1. Updating the incident response playbooks to include specific steps for detecting and containing ransomware infections.
2. Modifying the security monitoring rules and alerts to detect the indicators of compromise (IOCs) associated with the new ransomware variant.
3. Prioritizing the patching and hardening of systems and applications that are vulnerable to ransomware exploits.
4. Conducting targeted threat-hunting exercises to identify and remediate any potential ransomware infections proactively.
5. Engaging with industry peers and sharing threat intelligence to defend against the ransomware campaign collaboratively.

By continuously adapting incident response strategies based on the evolving threat landscape, GenAI can help organizations maintain a proactive and resilient security posture. Instead of relying on static and reactive incident response approaches, organizations can leverage the power of GenAI to dynamically adjust their detection, investigation, and mitigation tactics in real time, staying one step ahead of the adversaries.

Moreover, GenAI can automate certain incident response actions based on the adapted strategies. For example, suppose the GenAI model detects a high-confidence indicator of an ongoing data exfiltration attempt. In that case, it can automatically trigger a predefined playbook to isolate the compromised system, block the malicious traffic, and initiate a forensic investigation. This can help to reduce the mean time to respond (MTTR) and minimize the potential impact of security incidents.

However, adapting incident response strategies based on GenAI-generated insights presents certain challenges and considerations.

One challenge is the need for robust and reliable threat intelligence data to train and update the GenAI models. Organizations must establish processes and partnerships to continuously collect, validate, and enrich threat intelligence from multiple sources, ensuring the quality and relevance of the data fed into the GenAI models.

Another challenge is the potential for false positives or false negatives in the GenAI-generated adaptations. As with any AI-based system, the models risk making incorrect or biased decisions based on incomplete or noisy data. To mitigate these risks, it is important to incorporate human oversight and validation into the adaptation process, allowing security experts to review and approve the recommended changes before implementing them in production environments.

Despite these challenges, GenAI's promise of automating incident response and remediation is significant. GenAI can enable organizations to create dynamic and adaptive incident response strategies to keep pace with the ever-evolving threat landscape by leveraging the power of generative models and real-time threat intelligence. As GenAI techniques advance, we expect to see even more sophisticated and effective approaches to incident response automation, empowering organizations to build resilient and proactive defense capabilities against the most persistent and advanced cyber threats.

3.3 Improving Vulnerability Management and Risk Assessment

Vulnerability management and risk assessment are critical processes in cybersecurity that involve identifying, evaluating, and prioritizing security weaknesses in an organization's systems, networks, and applications. Traditional approaches to vulnerability management often rely on manual and periodic assessments, which can be time-consuming, resource-intensive, and reactive. GenAI can revolutionize vulnerability management and risk assessment by enabling the generation of proactive attack scenarios and prioritizing vulnerabilities based on their exploitability and impact.

3.3.1 Generating attack scenarios for proactive vulnerability assessment

One key challenge in vulnerability management is identifying and assessing security weaknesses before attackers can exploit them. While traditional vulnerability scanning tools can help identify known vulnerabilities based on predefined signatures and rules, they often fail to uncover complex or chained vulnerabilities that may arise from the interactions between different systems, components, or configurations.

GenAI can address this challenge by generating realistic and diverse attack scenarios that can help to identify and assess potential vulnerabilities proactively. By training on a large corpus of historical attack data, threat intelligence reports, and vulnerability databases, GenAI models, such as generative adversarial networks (GANs) or variational autoencoders (VAEs), can learn the common patterns, techniques, and exploit chains used by attackers.

For example, a GAN-based attack scenario generation model can be trained on a dataset of past cyber incidents, learning the typical attack vectors, tactics, and objectives employed by different threat actors. The model can then generate new, unseen attack scenarios that mimic the behavior and characteristics of real-world attacks but with unique variations and combinations of vulnerabilities and exploits.

These generated attack scenarios can be used to conduct proactive and targeted vulnerability assessments, simulating the actions of potential attackers and identifying weaknesses that may not be apparent through traditional scanning methods. By exposing systems and applications to a wide range of realistic attack scenarios, organizations can uncover hidden vulnerabilities, misconfigurations, or security gaps that adversaries could exploit.

Moreover, GenAI-based attack scenario generation can be customized and adapted to an organization's specific context and requirements. For instance, the models can be trained on industry-specific threat intelligence or tailored to the organization's technology stack, security policies, and risk appetite. This can help generate more relevant and actionable attack scenarios that reflect the organization's unique challenges and priorities.

However, ensuring that the generated attack scenarios are properly validated and tested is important to avoid false positives or unrealistic assumptions. Security experts should review and test the scenarios in controlled environments to verify their feasibility and potential impact. The generated scenarios should also be used with other vulnerability assessment techniques, such as penetration testing or code review, to provide a comprehensive and multi-layered approach to identifying and mitigating vulnerabilities.

3.3.2 Prioritizing Vulnerabilities based on Exploitability and Impact

Another key challenge in vulnerability management is prioritizing the remediation of identified vulnerabilities based on their criticality and potential impact. With the growing number and complexity of vulnerabilities discovered each year, organizations often need help determining which vulnerabilities should be addressed first, given limited resources and competing priorities.

GenAI can help to prioritize vulnerabilities by learning to assess their exploitability and potential impact based on various factors, such as the ease of exploitation, the availability of exploit code, the prevalence of vulnerable systems, and the potential consequences of a successful attack. GenAI models can learn to predict the likelihood and severity of training on a large corpus of vulnerability data, exploit databases, and impact vulnerabilities being exploited in the wild by assessments.

For example, a GenAI-based vulnerability prioritization model can be trained on a dataset of historical vulnerability disclosures, exploit code repositories, and security incident reports. The model can learn to identify the common characteristics and indicators of highly exploitable and impactful vulnerabilities, such as:

1. The existence of public exploit code or proof-of-concept (PoC)

demonstrations.
2. The presence of vulnerable systems or applications in popular software products or platforms.
3. The ease of exploitation includes the lack of complex prerequisites or the ability to exploit remotely.
4. The potential impact of exploitation, such as the ability to gain unauthorized access, execute arbitrary code, or cause system downtime.
5. The criticality of affected systems or data, such as those related to mission-critical operations, sensitive information, or regulatory compliance.

Based on these learned patterns and indicators, the GenAI model can generate risk scores or prioritization rankings for newly discovered vulnerabilities, helping organizations focus their remediation efforts on the most critical and pressing security issues.

Moreover, GenAI-based vulnerability prioritization can be continuously updated and refined based on real-time threat intelligence and exploit activity data. As new vulnerabilities are disclosed or new exploit techniques are observed in the wild, the models can learn to adapt their prioritization criteria and risk assessments, ensuring that organizations can stay ahead of the evolving threat landscape.

However, prioritizing vulnerabilities based on GenAI-generated risk scores also presents challenges and considerations. One challenge is the potential for biased or incomplete data used to train the models, which may lead to skewed or inaccurate prioritization outcomes. To mitigate these risks, it is important to ensure the training data's diversity, quality, and representativeness, incorporating multiple sources of vulnerability and exploiting intelligence.

Another challenge is human oversight and contextual understanding in the prioritization process. While GenAI models can provide valuable insights and recommendations, the final prioritization decisions should be made by security experts who can consider the specific business, operational, and technical factors relevant to the organization. The GenAI-generated risk scores should be treated as decision support tools rather than absolute truths, allowing human judgment and expertise to guide the remediation strategy.

Despite these challenges, the promise of GenAI in improving vulnerability management and risk assessment is significant. By leveraging the power of generative models and machine learning, GenAI can enable organizations to proactively identify and prioritize vulnerabilities based on realistic attack scenarios and data-driven risk assessments. As GenAI techniques advance, we can expect to see even more sophisticated and effective approaches to vulnerability management, empowering organizations to build stronger and more resilient security postures against the ever-evolving threat landscape.

3.4 Streamlining Security Operations and Reducing Human Error

Security operations teams monitor, detect, and respond to security events and incidents within an organization's IT environment. However, the increasing volume, velocity, and complexity of security data and the shortage of skilled security professionals can make it challenging for teams to manage and prioritize their workload effectively.

Moreover, the reliance on manual and repetitive tasks can lead to human errors, inconsistencies, and burnout among security analysts. GenAI has the potential to streamline security operations and reduce human error by automating repetitive tasks and augmenting human decision-making with data-driven insights.

3.4.1 Automating repetitive security tasks with GenAI

One key opportunity for GenAI in security operations is automating repetitive and time-consuming tasks that can be easily codified and delegated to intelligent systems. By training on large amounts of historical security data, workflows, and expert knowledge, GenAI models can learn to perform various security tasks accurately and efficiently, freeing human analysts to focus on more complex and strategic activities.

Some examples of security tasks that can be automated with GenAI include:

1. Alert triage and prioritization: GenAI models can learn to automatically classify and prioritize security alerts based on their severity, relevance, and potential impact, helping analysts to identify and respond to the most critical incidents quickly. By analyzing various contextual factors, such as asset criticality, threat intelligence, and user behavior, GenAI can provide risk-based recommendations for alert handling and escalation.

2. Security incident investigation: GenAI can assist in investigating security incidents by automatically collecting, correlating, and analyzing relevant data from multiple sources, such as system logs, network traffic, and endpoint telemetry. By learning the common patterns and indicators of compromise (IoCs) associated with different types of incidents, GenAI can help to speed up the root cause analysis and identify the scope and impact of the incident.

3. **Threat hunting and detection:** GenAI can automate the detection of advanced and unknown threats by learning the normal behavior of users, devices, and applications within an organization's environment. By continuously monitoring for anomalies and deviations from the learned baseline, GenAI can identify potential signs of malicious activity, such as unusual network connections, suspicious process executions, or abnormal resource usage.

4. **Security policy management:** GenAI can help automate the creation, implementation, and enforcement of security policies across an organization's IT infrastructure. By learning from existing policies, best practices, and regulatory requirements, GenAI models can generate optimized and consistent policy configurations for various security controls, such as firewalls, intrusion prevention systems (IPS), and access control lists (ACLs).

By automating these repetitive security tasks with GenAI, organizations can achieve several benefits, such as increased efficiency, reduced response times, and improved consistency in security operations. Moreover, the automation of low-level tasks can help alleviate the workload and stress on security analysts, allowing them to focus on more strategic and proactive activities, such as threat hunting, incident response planning, and security architecture design.

However, it is important to note that the automation of security tasks with GenAI should be implemented with proper governance, oversight, and human-in-the-loop controls. The GenAI models should be regularly tested, validated, and updated to ensure their accuracy, reliability, and alignment with the organization's security policies and objectives. Additionally, the automated actions should be logged, audited, and reviewed by human experts to maintain accountability and detect any potential errors or unintended consequences.

3.4.2 Augmenting human decision-making with GenAI Insights

Another key opportunity for GenAI in security operations is augmenting human decision-making insights and recommendations. While automation can help streamline repetitive tasks, many complex and contextual security decisions with data drive require human judgment, expertise, and creativity. GenAI can assist human analysts in making more informed and effective decisions by providing them with relevant, timely, and actionable insights based on large-scale data analysis and machine learning.

Some examples of how GenAI can augment human decision-making in security operations include:

1. Contextual threat intelligence: GenAI models can learn to extract and synthesize relevant threat intelligence from various internal and external sources, such as security blogs, social media, dark web forums, and threat intelligence feeds. By providing human analysts with real-time and contextual threat information, such as emerging attack tactics, vulnerabilities, and indicators of compromise (IoCs), GenAI can

3. THE PROMISE OF GENAI IN CYBERSECURITY

help them to make more proactive and targeted decisions for threat detection, hunting, and response.

2. Risk-based prioritization: GenAI can assist human analysts in prioritizing security events, vulnerabilities, and incidents based on their potential risk and impact on the organization. By learning from historical incident data, asset criticality, and business context, GenAI models can generate risk scores and recommendations that help analysts focus their attention and resources on the most significant and urgent security issues.

3. Adaptive security policy recommendations: GenAI can provide human analysts with adaptive and context-aware recommendations for security policy configurations and controls. By analyzing various factors, such as the organization's risk profile, compliance requirements, and user behavior patterns, GenAI models can suggest optimized and dynamic security policies that balance security, usability, and productivity.

4. Collaborative incident response: GenAI can facilitate collaboration and knowledge sharing among security analysts during incident response and investigations. By learning from the collective expertise and actions of multiple analysts across different incidents, GenAI models can provide guided recommendations and best practices for incident handling based on similar past experiences and successful response strategies.

By augmenting human decision-making with GenAI insights, security operations teams can make more informed, consistent, and effective decisions in the face of complex and evolving security challenges. Combining human expertise and machine intelligence can lead to faster incident detection and response, improved risk management, and better alignment of security practices with business objectives.

However, it is important to recognize that GenAI insights should be treated as decision support rather than decision replacement. Human analysts should always maintain the final authority and accountability for security decisions, using their judgment and experience to validate and contextualize the GenAI recommendations. Moreover, the GenAI models should be designed with transparency, explainability, and human oversight, allowing analysts to understand and trust the reasoning behind the generated insights.

Another consideration is the potential for bias and errors in GenAI-generated insights, which can arise from biased or incomplete training data, flawed assumptions, or concept drift over time. To mitigate these risks, ensuring the diversity, quality, and representativeness of the data used to train the GenAI models and regularly monitoring, testing, and updating them based on feedback and performance metrics is important.

Despite these challenges, GenAI's promise to streamline security operations and reduce human error is significant. By leveraging the power of automation and augmentation, GenAI can help organizations build more efficient, effective, and resilient security operations centers (SOCs) that can keep pace with the ever-evolving threat landscape. As GenAI techniques advance, we expect to see even more innovative and impactful applications, enabling human analysts to make better decisions and focus on higher-valuing security operations activities that require their unique skills and expertise.

4. The Perils of GenAI in Cybersecurity

While the potential benefits of GenAI in cybersecurity are significant, it is equally important to acknowledge and address the potential risks and challenges associated with its adoption. One of the major concerns surrounding the use of GenAI in cybersecurity is the issue of bias and fairness in the models and their outputs. Biased GenAI systems can lead to inaccurate, discriminatory, and harmful decisions that undermine the effectiveness and trustworthiness of cybersecurity solutions. This section will explore the types of biases that can occur in GenAI models and their impact on cybersecurity decision-making.

4.1 Bias and Fairness Concerns

Bias in AI systems refers to systematic and unfair discrimination against certain individuals or groups based on their inherent characteristics or social identities, such as race, gender, age, or socioeconomic status. In the context of GenAI for cybersecurity, bias can manifest in various forms, leading to skewed or discriminatory outcomes that can seriously affect individuals, organizations, and society.

4.1.1 Types of biases in GenAI models

Two main types of biases can occur in GenAI models: data bias and algorithmic bias.

4.1.1.1 Data bias: unrepresentative or skewed training data

Data bias arises when the training data used to develop GenAI models is unrepresentative, imbalanced, or skewed toward certain groups or characteristics. This can happen due to various reasons, such as:

1. **Historical bias:** The training data may reflect historical biases, prejudices, or discriminatory practices that exist in the real world, such as the underrepresentation of certain demographic groups in cybersecurity roles or the over-policing of certain communities.

2. **Selection bias:** Collecting, selecting, and curating training data may introduce biases, such as oversampling certain security events or excluding certain data sources or perspectives.

3. **Measurement bias:** How data is measured, labeled, or annotated may introduce biases, such as the subjective interpretation of security incidents or the inconsistent application of severity ratings.

When GenAI models are trained on biased data, they can learn and perpetuate these biases in their outputs, leading to unfair or discriminatory decisions. For example, a GenAI model trained on historical cyber threat data that overrepresents certain geographic regions or industry sectors may generate biased threat intelligence that disproportionately targets or stigmatizes those groups.

4.1.1.2 Algorithmic bias: biases introduced by model architectures or optimization

Algorithmic bias occurs when the design, architecture, or optimization of GenAI models introduces biases not present in the training data. This can happen due to various factors, such as:

1. Model assumptions: The assumptions and simplifications made in designing GenAI models, such as the choice of input features, output variables, or objective functions, can introduce biases that favor certain outcomes or groups over others.

2. Model complexity: The complexity and opacity of some GenAI models, such as deep neural networks, can make it difficult to identify and mitigate biases that may emerge from the interactions between different layers and parameters.

3. Optimization criteria: The criteria used to optimize GenAI models, such as the choice of loss functions, regularization terms, or hyperparameters, can introduce biases that prioritize certain performance metrics over others, such as accuracy over fairness.

Algorithmic bias can lead to GenAI models that make unfair or discriminatory decisions, even when trained on unbiased data. For example, a GenAI model optimized for minimizing false positives in malware detection may inadvertently introduce racial or socioeconomic biases by flagging more benign files from certain user groups as malicious.

4.1.2 Impact of biased GenAI on cybersecurity decision-making

The biases present in GenAI models can have significant and harmful impacts on cybersecurity decision-making, both at the individual and systemic levels.

4.1.2.1 False positives and false negatives in threat detection

Biased GenAI models can lead to higher rates of false positives and false negatives in threat detection and classification. False positives occur when benign activities or entities are incorrectly flagged as malicious, while false negatives occur when actual threats are missed or overlooked. The consequences of these errors can be severe, such as:

1. **Wasted resources:** False positives can lead to the unnecessary allocation of time, effort, and resources to investigate and respond to non-existent threats, diverting attention away from real security issues.

2. **Decreased productivity:** False positives can disrupt normal business operations and user workflows, as legitimate activities may be blocked, quarantined, or subjected to additional security measures.

3. **Missed threats:** False negatives can allow real threats to go undetected and unchecked, leading to successful attacks, data breaches, or other security incidents that can cause significant financial, reputational, and operational damage.

Biased GenAI models can exacerbate these problems by systematically generating false positives or false negatives for certain groups or characteristics, such as flagging more legitimate traffic from certain countries as malicious or overlooking threats targeting specific industry sectors.

4.1.2.2 Discriminatory impact on individuals or groups

Biased GenAI models can also have discriminatory impacts on individuals or groups, perpetuating or amplifying existing social inequalities and power imbalances. For example:

1. **Unequal protection:** Biased GenAI models may provide unequal levels of security protection to different user groups, such as prioritizing the monitoring and response to threats that affect more affluent or influential communities over those that impact marginalized or underserved populations.

2. **Discriminatory profiling:** Biased GenAI models may generate discriminatory risk profiles or threat assessments based on users' demographic characteristics, such as assigning higher risk scores to individuals from certain racial, ethnic, or religious backgrounds.

3. **Disparate treatment:** Biased GenAI models may lead to disparate treatment of individuals or groups in security decision-making, such as subjecting certain users to more invasive security measures, such as additional authentication requirements or access restrictions, based on their inherent attributes.

Biased GenAI models can have discriminatory impacts, erode public trust in cybersecurity systems, reinforce existing biases and stereotypes, and contribute to the marginalization and oppression of vulnerable communities. Moreover, using biased GenAI in high-stakes security contexts, such as law enforcement, national security, or critical infrastructure protection, can have far-reaching and devastating consequences for individuals and society.

To mitigate the risks of bias and discrimination in GenAI for cybersecurity, adopting a proactive and holistic approach that addresses both data and algorithmic biases is essential. This includes:

1. Ensuring training data's diversity, representativeness, and quality by including data from different sources, perspectives, and demographic groups and carefully curating and preprocessing the data to remove or mitigate existing biases.

2. Design and evaluate GenAI models with fairness and transparency in mind, incorporating fairness metrics and constraints into the optimization process, testing the models for disparate impact and treatment, and providing clear and interpretable explanations of the model outputs and decisions.

3. Establishing governance and accountability mechanisms for the development and deployment of GenAI in cybersecurity by involving diverse stakeholders and domain experts in the design and oversight of the models, conducting regular audits and assessments of the models' performance and fairness, and providing channels for users to challenge or appeal the decisions made by the models.

4. Promoting diversity, equity, and inclusion in the cybersecurity workforce and culture by increasing the representation and participation of underrepresented groups in the development and deployment of GenAI systems, providing training and education on issues of bias and

fairness, and fostering a culture of openness, empathy, and respect for diversity.

By proactively addressing the issues of bias and fairness in GenAI for cybersecurity, we can harness the power of these technologies to build more effective, trustworthy, and equitable security solutions that benefit all members of society. However, this requires ongoing vigilance, collaboration, and commitment from all stakeholders involved in the development and deployment of GenAI, including researchers, practitioners, policymakers, and the public.

4.1.2 Impact of biased GenAI on cybersecurity decision-making

The presence of biases in GenAI models can have severe consequences for cybersecurity decision-making. Biased models can lead to inaccurate, unfair, and harmful outcomes that undermine the effectiveness and trustworthiness of cybersecurity solutions. In this section, we will explore two main impacts of biased GenAI on cybersecurity decision-making: false positives and false negatives in threat detection and discriminatory impact on individuals or groups.

4.1.2.1 False positives and false negatives in threat detection

One of the primary applications of GenAI in cybersecurity is in threat detection and classification. GenAI models can be trained on large datasets of malware, network traffic, and system logs to identify patterns and anomalies that indicate potential security threats. However, when these models are biased, they can produce higher rates of false positives and false negatives, leading to serious consequences for organizations and individuals.

False positives occur when a GenAI model incorrectly identifies a benign activity or entity as malicious. For example, a biased model may flag legitimate network traffic from certain geographic regions or industry sectors as suspicious based on the overrepresentation of those attributes in the training data. False positives can have several negative impacts on cybersecurity decision-making, such as:

1. Resource waste: False positives can lead to the unnecessary allocation of time, effort, and resources to investigate and respond to non-existent threats. Security teams may spend hours or days analyzing and triaging alerts that turn out to be false alarms, diverting their attention from real security issues.

2. Productivity loss: False positives can disrupt normal business operations and user workflows. Legitimate activities, such as sending emails or accessing files, may be blocked, quarantined, or subjected to additional security measures, causing frustration and productivity loss for users.

3. Alert fatigue: High rates of false positives can lead to alert fatigue among security analysts, who may become desensitized to the constant stream of alerts and start ignoring or dismissing them altogether. This can create a dangerous situation where real threats are missed or overlooked, increasing the risk of successful attacks.

On the other hand, false negatives occur when a GenAI model fails to detect or classify an actual threat. For example, a biased model may overlook certain types of malware or attack vectors underrepresented in the training data, allowing them to evade detection and cause harm. False negatives can have even more severe consequences than false positives, such as:

1. **Missed attacks:** False negatives can allow real threats to go undetected and unchecked, leading to successful attacks, data breaches, or other security incidents. Attackers may exploit the gaps in the GenAI models to launch targeted or stealthy attacks that bypass traditional security controls.

2. **Delayed response:** Even if a threat is eventually detected, false negatives can delay the response and mitigation efforts, giving attackers more time to cause damage or exfiltrate data. The longer a threat remains undetected, the more difficult and costly it becomes to contain and eradicate it.

3. **Compliance violations:** False negatives can lead to violations of security and privacy regulations, such as GDPR, HIPAA, or PCI-DSS. These regulations require organizations to detect and report security incidents promptly. Failure to do so can result in legal liabilities, financial penalties, and reputational damage.

The impact of false positives and false negatives on cybersecurity decision-making is not just a technical issue but also a human one. Security analysts and incident responders rely on the outputs of GenAI models to make critical decisions about which threats to prioritize, investigate, and mitigate. When these outputs are biased or inaccurate, they can lead to poor decisions that put organizations and individuals at risk.

To mitigate the impact of biased GenAI on threat detection, it is essential to:

1. Ensure the quality and diversity of training data by including a representative sample of threats, attack vectors, and benign activities and continuously update the data to reflect the evolving threat landscape.

2. Validate and test the GenAI models for accuracy, fairness, and robustness using a combination of statistical metrics, domain expertise, and adversarial testing techniques and monitoring the models' performance and outputs in production.

3. Explain the model outputs clearly and interpretably using feature importance, counterfactual analysis, and rule extraction techniques to help security analysts understand and trust the models' decisions.

4. Combine GenAI with human expertise and context by involving security analysts in developing and deploying the models, providing them with the necessary training and tools to interpret and act on the model outputs and fostering a culture of collaboration and continuous improvement.

4.1.2.2 Discriminatory impact on individuals or groups

Another major concern with biased GenAI in cybersecurity is the potential for discriminatory impact on individuals or groups. When GenAI models are trained on biased data or designed with biased assumptions, they can perpetuate or amplify existing social inequalities and power imbalances, leading to unfair or harmful outcomes for certain population segments.

For example, a biased GenAI model used for user profiling and risk

4. THE PERILS OF GENAI IN CYBERSECURITY

assessment may assign higher risk scores to individuals from certain racial, ethnic, or socioeconomic backgrounds based on historical biases in the criminal justice system or the cybersecurity industry. This can lead to discriminatory treatment of these individuals, such as subjecting them to more frequent or invasive security screenings, denying them access to certain resources or services, or flagging their activities as suspicious or malicious.

The discriminatory impact of biased GenAI can have serious consequences for individuals and communities, such as:

1. Reinforcing stereotypes: Biased GenAI models can reinforce and perpetuate harmful stereotypes and prejudices about certain groups, such as associating certain cyber threats with particular nationalities, religions, or political ideologies. This can lead to stigmatization, marginalization, and discrimination of these groups, both online and offline.

2. Limiting opportunities: Biased GenAI models can limit the opportunities and freedoms of individuals from certain backgrounds by denying them access to education, employment, or other resources based on their perceived risk or threat level. This can create a vicious cycle of exclusion and disadvantage that is difficult to break.

3. Violating civil liberties: Biased GenAI models can violate individuals' civil liberties and human rights by subjecting them to unwarranted surveillance, censorship, or punishment based on their inherent characteristics or social identities. This can churn out free speech, privacy, and other fundamental freedoms.

4. Eroding trust: Using biased GenAI in cybersecurity can erode public trust in the fairness and integrity of security systems, leading to a breakdown of social cohesion and cooperation. When individuals feel they are being unfairly targeted or discriminated against by security measures, they may be less likely to comply with them or report suspicious activities.

To mitigate the discriminatory impact of biased GenAI, it is essential to adopt a holistic and proactive approach that addresses both technical and social aspects of the problem. This includes:

1. Conducting bias and fairness audits of GenAI models using techniques such as disparate impact analysis, sensitivity analysis, and ethical matrix to identify and mitigate potential sources of bias and discrimination.

2. Ensuring diverse and inclusive representation in developing and deploying GenAI models by involving individuals from different backgrounds, perspectives, and experiences in the models' design, testing, and oversight.

3. Providing transparency and accountability for GenAI decisions by making the models and their outputs open to public scrutiny and feedback, establishing clear processes for individuals to challenge or appeal the decisions made by the models, and holding the developers and deployers of the models responsible for their outcomes.

4. Promoting digital literacy and critical thinking skills among the general public by educating individuals about the potential biases and limitations of GenAI models, empowering them to question and challenge the decisions made by these models, and fostering a culture of healthy skepticism and dialogue around the use of AI in cybersecurity.

Addressing the discriminatory impact of biased GenAI in cybersecurity is not just a technical challenge but also a social and ethical one. It requires a collaborative and multidisciplinary approach that brings together computer science, social science, law, and ethics experts and the affected communities and stakeholders. Only by working together can we ensure that the benefits of GenAI in cybersecurity are distributed fairly and equitably and that the risks and harms are minimized and mitigated.

4.2 Explainability and Interpretability Challenges

One of the major challenges in applying GenAI to cybersecurity is the issue of explainability and interpretability. Explainability refers to the ability to understand and explain how a GenAI model arrives at its decisions or outputs, while interpretability refers to the ability to interpret the meaning and significance of those decisions or outputs in the context of the specific cybersecurity task or domain. The lack of explainability and interpretability in GenAI models can create significant challenges for cybersecurity professionals, who need to be able to trust, validate, and act upon the insights and recommendations provided by these models. This section will explore the "black box" problem in GenAI and its implications for cybersecurity.

4.2.1 The "black box" problem in GenAI

The "black box" problem refers to the opacity and complexity of many GenAI models, particularly those based on deep learning architectures such as neural networks. These models can have millions or billions of parameters and complex, non-linear interactions between their inputs and outputs, making it difficult for humans to understand how they arrive at their decisions or predictions. The lack of transparency and interpretability in these models can create several challenges for cybersecurity, which we will discuss in more detail below.

4.2.1.1 Difficulty in understanding complex GenAI model decisions

One of the main challenges of the "black box" problem in GenAI is the difficulty in understanding how these models make their decisions or predictions. Unlike traditional rule-based or statistical models with clear and explicit decision logic, GenAI models learn to make decisions based on complex patterns and relationships in the data, which may not be easily understandable or explainable to humans.

For example, a GenAI model trained to detect malware may learn to identify certain features or combinations of features in the malware code that predict malicious behavior. Still, these features may not be easily interpretable or meaningful to human analysts. The model may also learn to make decisions based on subtle or non-intuitive patterns in the data, such as the order or frequency of certain API calls or the presence of specific byte sequences, which may be difficult for humans to discern or reason about.

The difficulty in understanding GenAI model decisions can create several challenges for cybersecurity professionals, such as:

1. Lack of trust: When cybersecurity professionals cannot understand or explain how a GenAI model arrives at its decisions, they may be less likely to trust or act upon those decisions, particularly in high-stakes situations where the consequences of a false positive or false negative can be severe.

2. **Difficulty in validation:** Without a clear understanding of how a GenAI model makes its decisions, it can be difficult for cybersecurity professionals to validate or verify the correctness or appropriateness of those decisions, particularly in the face of evolving threats or changing environmental conditions.

3. **Limited ability to improve:** When the decision logic of a GenAI model is opaque or difficult to understand, it can be challenging for cybersecurity professionals to identify and correct errors or biases in the model or to adapt the model to new or unexpected situations.

4. **Regulatory and legal challenges:** In some domains, such as finance or healthcare, there may be regulatory or legal requirements for the explainability and interpretability of AI models used in decision-making. The lack of transparency in GenAI models may make it difficult for organizations to comply with these requirements or to defend their use of these models in the event of an audit or lawsuit.

To address these challenges, researchers and practitioners in the field of explainable AI (XAI) have developed a range of techniques and approaches for improving the interpretability and transparency of GenAI models. These include:

1. **Feature importance:** Techniques such as permutation importance or SHAP (SHapley Additive exPlanations) can be used to identify the input features that have the greatest influence on a GenAI model's decisions or outputs, helping to provide some insight into the model's decision logic.

2. Visualization: Techniques such as activation maps or saliency maps can visualize the patterns or regions in the input data most important for a GenAI model's decisions, providing a more intuitive and human-understandable representation of the model's behavior.

3. Rule extraction: Techniques such as decision trees or rule induction can extract simplified, human-readable rules or decision paths from a trained GenAI model, providing a more transparent and interpretable representation of the model's decision logic.

4. Counterfactual explanations: Techniques such as contrastive explanations or adversarial examples can generate alternative inputs or scenarios that would change a GenAI model's decision, helping to identify the key factors or features that influence the model's behavior.

While these techniques can help to improve the interpretability and transparency of GenAI models to some extent, they are not a complete solution to the "black box" problem, and there is still much work to be done in this area. In particular, there is a need for more research on effectively communicating and visualizing the decision logic of GenAI models to non-technical stakeholders, such as business leaders or policymakers, who may not have a deep understanding of the underlying algorithms or data.

4.2.1.2 Lack of transparency in GenAI-based cybersecurity systems

Another major challenge of the "black box" problem in GenAI is the lack of transparency in the overall cybersecurity systems and workflows that incorporate these models. Even if individual GenAI models can be made more interpretable or explainable, the complex interactions and dependencies between these models and other components of

4. THE PERILS OF GENAI IN CYBERSECURITY

the cybersecurity system can still create significant challenges for transparency and accountability.

For example, a GenAI-based intrusion detection system may rely on different models and data sources, such as network traffic analysis, user behavior analytics, and threat intelligence feeds, to identify potential security threats. Each of these models may have its own "black box" decision logic, and how these models are combined and integrated into the overall system may not be easily understandable or explainable to human operators.

The lack of transparency in GenAI-based cybersecurity systems can create several challenges, such as:

1. **Difficulty in troubleshooting:** When a GenAI-based cybersecurity system generates an alert or takes action, it can be difficult for human operators to understand the underlying reasons or factors that led to that decision, making it challenging to troubleshoot or investigate potential false positives or false negatives.

2. **Limited situational awareness:** The lack of transparency in GenAI-based cybersecurity systems can limit the situational awareness of human operators, who may not clearly understand the system's current state or context or the potential risks or vulnerabilities it is detecting or mitigating.

3. **Difficulty in auditing and compliance:** The opacity of GenAI-based cybersecurity systems can make it difficult for organizations to audit or verify their effectiveness and compliance, particularly in regulated industries or domains where strict requirements for transparency and accountability exist.

4. Erosion of trust: The lack of transparency in GenAI-based cybersecurity systems can erode the trust of users and stakeholders, particularly if high-profile failures or incidents highlight these models' limitations or biases.

To address these challenges, there is a need for more research and development on techniques and approaches for improving the transparency and accountability of GenAI-based cybersecurity systems. This may include:

1. System-level explanations: Techniques for generating high-level, human-understandable explanations of the overall behavior and decision-making of GenAI-based cybersecurity systems, considering the interactions and dependencies between different models and components.

2. Provenance and lineage: Techniques for tracking and documenting the provenance and lineage of data and models used in GenAI-based cybersecurity systems, providing a clear audit trail of how these systems were developed, trained, and deployed.

3. Human-in-the-loop approaches: Techniques for integrating human expertise and oversight into the decision-making processes of GenAI-based cybersecurity systems, allowing human operators to review, validate, and override these systems' decisions or actions when necessary.

4. Transparency and accountability frameworks: The development of standardized frameworks and best practices for ensuring the transparency and accountability of GenAI-based cybersecurity systems, including guidelines for documentation, testing, and validation.

Addressing the challenges of explainability and interpretability in GenAI-based cybersecurity systems will require a collaborative and interdisciplinary effort, bringing together experts from AI, cybersecurity, human-computer interaction, and other relevant fields. It will also require ongoing engagement and dialogue with stakeholders and end-users of these systems to ensure that the solutions developed are practical, usable, and aligned with the needs and expectations of the cybersecurity community.

Ultimately, improving the explainability and interpretability of GenAI-based cybersecurity systems aims to satisfy regulatory or compliance requirements and enhance the effectiveness, trustworthiness, and accountability of these systems in protecting against evolving cyber threats. By providing greater transparency and insight into the decision-making processes of these systems, we can empower human operators to make more informed and effective decisions and work in closer collaboration with AI-based tools and technologies to achieve better cybersecurity outcomes.

4.2.2 Importance of explainable AI in cybersecurity

The importance of explainable AI (XAI) in cybersecurity cannot be overstated. GenAI models become increasingly complex and opaque, and the need for techniques and approaches to provide clarity, transparency, and accountability in their decision-making processes becomes ever more critical. This section will explore why explainable AI is essential for building trust and accountability in GenAI-based cybersecurity systems.

4.2.2.1 Building trust and accountability

One of the primary reasons explainable AI is so important in cybersecurity is that it helps build trust and accountability in using GenAI models. Trust is essential in any cybersecurity context, as organizations and individuals must be confident that the tools and technologies they rely on to protect their assets and data are effective, reliable, and aligned with their values and objectives. Accountability is equally important, as it ensures that the developers, operators, and users of GenAI-based cybersecurity systems are held responsible for the decisions and actions of these systems and that there are clear mechanisms in place for identifying and correcting errors, biases, or unintended consequences.

There are several ways in which explainable AI can help to build trust and accountability in GenAI-based cybersecurity systems:

1. **Providing transparency:** Explainable AI techniques can provide greater transparency into the decision-making processes of GenAI models, allowing stakeholders to understand how these models arrive at their outputs or recommendations. This transparency is essential for building trust, as it allows stakeholders to verify that the models are operating as intended and that their decisions are based on valid and relevant factors.

2. **Enabling auditability:** Explainable AI techniques can enable better auditability of GenAI-based cybersecurity systems by providing clear and comprehensive records of the data, algorithms, and processes used in these systems. This auditability is critical for accountability, as it allows stakeholders to investigate and assess these systems' performance and compliance and identify and correct any issues or errors.

3. **Facilitating human oversight:** Explainable AI techniques can facilitate human oversight and control over GenAI-based cybersecurity systems by providing human operators with the information and tools they need to understand, interpret, and override the decisions of these systems when necessary. This human oversight is essential for building trust and accountability, as it ensures that there is always a human in the loop who can take responsibility for the actions and outcomes of these systems.

4. **Supporting legal and regulatory compliance:** Explainable AI techniques can support legal and regulatory compliance using GenAI-based cybersecurity systems by providing the documentation, evidence, and explanations required by relevant laws, standards, and guidelines. This compliance is critical for accountability, as it ensures that organizations using these systems meet their legal and ethical obligations and can demonstrate this compliance to regulators, auditors, and other stakeholders.

5. **Enhancing collaboration and communication:** Explainable AI techniques can enhance collaboration and communication between the stakeholders involved in developing, deploying, and using GenAI-based cybersecurity systems by providing a common language and framework for discussing and understanding the behavior and performance of these systems. This collaboration and communication is essential for building trust and accountability, as it ensures that all stakeholders have a shared understanding of the goals, limitations, and potential risks of these systems and that they can work together to optimize their effectiveness and mitigate any negative impacts.

To illustrate the importance of explainable AI for building trust and accountability in GenAI-based cybersecurity systems, consider the following scenario:

Suppose a financial institution has deployed a GenAI-based fraud detection system to monitor its customers' transactions and identify potential fraudulent activity. The system uses a complex deep learning model trained on a large dataset of historical transaction data, generating real-time alerts and recommendations for investigating and responding to suspected fraud cases.

However, the system's decision-making process is largely opaque, and the fraud analysts responsible for reviewing and acting on its alerts do not understand how the model arrives at its predictions or what factors it considers in its analysis. This lack of explainability creates several challenges for trust and accountability:

- The fraud analysts may not trust the system's recommendations, as they cannot verify that the model makes decisions based on valid and relevant factors. This lack of trust may lead to a high rate of false positives, as the analysts may feel compelled to investigate every alert, even if they are not confident in the system's accuracy.
- The financial institution may struggle to demonstrate compliance with relevant regulations and standards, such as the EU's General Data Protection Regulation (GDPR) or the Payment Card Industry Data Security Standard (PCI DSS), which require organizations to provide explanations and justifications for automated decision-making systems that significantly impact individuals.
- Suppose the system makes an incorrect prediction that leads to a customer being wrongly accused of fraud or having their account frozen. In that case, the financial institution may face legal and reputational challenges. It will be difficult to determine how the error occurred or who is responsible for the harm caused to the

customer.

The financial institution could deploy explainable AI techniques to address these challenges and provide greater transparency and accountability in the fraud detection system. For example:

- The system could use feature importance techniques, such as SHAP or LIME, to identify the key factors contributing to each fraud prediction and present these factors to the fraud analysts in a clear and understandable format. This would allow the analysts to understand the reasoning behind each alert better and make more informed decisions about which cases to prioritize for investigation.
- The system could generate counterfactual explanations for each fraud prediction, showing how the prediction would change if certain input features were modified. This would help the analysts identify potential false positives and understand the model's sensitivity to different types of transaction data.
- The system could maintain detailed logs and audit trails of all the data, algorithms, and processes used in each fraud prediction, allowing the financial institution to demonstrate compliance with relevant regulations and to investigate and correct any errors or biases in the model.
- The system could include human-in-the-loop mechanisms, such as manual review thresholds or override procedures, to ensure that the fraud analysts can review and validate the model's predictions before taking any actions that could impact customers.

By implementing these explainable AI techniques, the financial institution could build greater trust and accountability in its fraud detection system, internally among its analysts and externally among its customers and regulators. This would ultimately lead to a more effective and reliable system that can better protect the institution and its stakeholders from the risks of financial fraud.

4.2.2.2 Enabling human oversight and intervention

Another key reason AI is important in cybersecurity is that it enables human oversight and intervention when using GenAI-based systems. While GenAI models can be incredibly powerful tools for detecting and responding to cyber threats, they are not infallible, and there will always be situations where human judgment and expertise are required to make critical decisions or to take appropriate actions.

Explainable AI techniques can enable this human oversight and intervention by providing human operators with the information and tools they need to understand, interpret, and act upon the outputs of GenAI models. This is particularly important in high-stakes cybersecurity contexts, such as incident response or threat hunting, where the consequences of false positives or false negatives can be severe and where human operators need to quickly and accurately assess the situational context and determine the most appropriate course of action.

There are several ways in which explainable AI can enable human oversight and intervention in GenAI-based cybersecurity systems:

1. Providing situational awareness: Explainable AI techniques can give human operators greater situational awareness of the current state and context of the cybersecurity environment by presenting relevant information and insights from GenAI models in a clear and understandable format. This situational awareness is critical for enabling human operators to make informed decisions and to take appropriate actions in response to evolving threats or incidents.

2. Supporting decision-making: Explainable AI techniques can support human decision-making in cybersecurity by providing operators with the necessary context, evidence, and justifications for the outputs of GenAI models. This can include presenting the key factors contributing to a particular threat prediction, showing the potential impact or likelihood of different response options, or highlighting any uncertainties or limitations in the model's analysis.

3. Enabling manual overrides: Explainable AI techniques can enable human operators to manually override or adjust the decisions of GenAI models when necessary by allowing them to review and validate the model's outputs before taking any actions. This manual override capability ensures that human judgment and expertise can be applied when the model may be uncertain, biased, or misaligned with the operator's goals and priorities.

4. Facilitating collaboration: Explainable AI techniques can facilitate collaboration between human operators and GenAI models by providing a common language and framework for communication and coordination. This collaboration is critical for enabling human operators to leverage the strengths of GenAI models, such as their ability to process large amounts of data and identify complex patterns, while also being able to apply their domain knowledge and intuition to guide and refine the model's analysis.

5. Enabling continuous learning: Explainable AI techniques can enable continuous learning and improvement of GenAI-based cybersecurity systems by allowing human operators to review and provide feedback on the model's performance over time. This feedback can be used to retrain and update the model, ensuring it remains accurate, relevant, and aligned with the organization's evolving needs and priorities.

To illustrate the importance of explainable AI for enabling human oversight and intervention in GenAI-based cybersecurity systems, consider the following scenario:

Suppose that a SOC (Security Operations Center) team uses a GenAI-based threat detection system to monitor the organization's network traffic and identify potential indicators of compromise (IOCs). The system uses deep learning models to analyze various data sources, such as network flow logs, endpoint telemetry, and threat intelligence feeds. It generates real-time alerts and recommendations for investigation and response.

One day, the system generates a high-priority alert indicating that a critical server has been compromised and is communicating with a known command-and-control (C2) domain. The SOC analyst receiving the alert is initially skeptical, as the server in question is a well-secured and closely monitored system that has never been breached.

However, when the analyst examines the alert details using the system's explainable AI interface, they can see the key factors that contributed to the threat prediction, including:

- A sudden spike in network traffic between the server and the C2 domain is highly anomalous compared to the server's typical traffic patterns.
- Several known IOCs are associated with the C2 domain, including

malicious file hashes and IP addresses previously linked to cyber espionage campaigns.
- The use of encrypted communications and other evasive techniques that are consistent with advanced persistent threat (APT) activity.

Based on this information, the analyst can quickly confirm the threat's validity and initiate an incident response process to contain and investigate the compromise. The explainable AI interface also provides the analyst with recommended actions and procedures for isolating the affected server, collecting forensic evidence, and notifying relevant stakeholders.

As the incident response process unfolds, the explainable AI system provides the SOC team with real-time updates and insights, highlighting any new IOCs or detected anomalies and suggesting potential root causes and remediation options. The team can use this information to collaborate effectively with other IT and security personnel and make informed decisions about eradicating the threat and preventing future compromises.

In this scenario, the threat detection system's explainable AI capabilities enabled the SOC analyst to quickly and accurately assess the situational context, determine the appropriate response actions, and maintain oversight and control over the incident response process. Without these capabilities, the analyst may have been more likely to dismiss the alert as a false positive or struggle to coordinate an effective response due to a lack of visibility and understanding of the threat.

By providing transparent, interpretable, and actionable information to human operators, explainable AI techniques can thus enable more effective and reliable human oversight and intervention in GenAI-based cybersecurity systems. This is essential for ensuring that these systems are used in a responsible, accountable, and trustworthy manner and that human judgment and expertise can be applied to guide and enhance their performance in protecting against cyber threats.

4.3 Accountability and Ethical Considerations

As GenAI becomes increasingly integrated into cybersecurity systems and processes, it raises important questions about accountability and ethics. Who is responsible when a GenAI-based system makes a decision that leads to harm or damage? How can we ensure that these systems are being used ethically and responsibly and not perpetuate biases or discrimination? This section will explore these questions and consider the challenges and opportunities for ensuring accountability and ethics in using GenAI for cybersecurity.

4.3.1 Responsibility for GenAI-based decisions in cybersecurity

One key challenge in using GenAI for cybersecurity is determining who is responsible for the decisions and actions taken by these systems. Unlike traditional rule-based or manual security processes, where responsibility can be assigned to human operators or decision-makers, GenAI-based systems can operate autonomously. They can make decisions based on complex and opaque algorithms that their human users may not fully understand or control.

This lack of clear accountability can be particularly problematic when GenAI-based systems make incorrect or harmful decisions, such as false positives or false negatives in threat detection or inappropriate actions in automated incident response. In these cases, it may be difficult to determine who is liable for the resulting damages or harms and how to ensure appropriate corrective actions are taken to prevent future incidents.

4.3.1.1 Liability for false positives and false negatives

One area where responsibility and liability arise is in the case of false positives and negatives generated by GenAI-based threat detection systems. False positives occur when a system incorrectly identifies a benign activity or entity as malicious, while false negatives occur when a system fails to detect a genuine threat or attack.

Both false positives and negatives can seriously affect organizations and individuals. False positives can lead to wasted time and resources investigating and responding to non-existent threats and potential disruptions to legitimate business activities or user access. False negatives, on the other hand, can allow real attacks to go undetected and cause significant damage or data loss before they are discovered and contained.

In the case of false positives, the question of liability may depend on factors such as:

- The details of the false positive include the type of activity or entity incorrectly flagged and the potential impact or harm that could have resulted from the false positive.
- The design and implementation of the GenAI-based system, in-

cluding the quality and representativeness of the training data, the robustness and explainability of the algorithms, and the level of human oversight and control over the system's decisions.
- The contractual agreements and service level agreements (SLAs) between the organization using the GenAI-based system and any third-party vendors or service providers involved in its development or operation.
- The applicable legal and regulatory frameworks governing the use of AI in cybersecurity may vary depending on the jurisdiction and industry involved.

In general, liability for false positives may fall on the organization using the GenAI-based system, particularly if they have failed to properly configure, monitor, or validate the system's performance or used it in a way inconsistent with its intended purpose or capabilities. However, liability could also potentially extend to the developers or vendors of the GenAI-based system if it can be shown that the system was inherently flawed or biased in its design or implementation.

In the case of false negatives, the question of liability may be even more complex, as the failure to detect a genuine threat can result in significant harm or damage to the organization or its stakeholders. In these cases, liability may depend on factors such as:

- The severity and impact of the undetected threat, including the type of attack, the data or systems that were compromised, and the resulting financial, reputational, or regulatory consequences for the organization.
- The reasonableness of the organization's cybersecurity practices and controls, including its use of GenAI-based systems as part of a

broader security strategy and its adherence to industry standards and best practices for threat detection and response.
- The foreseeability of the specific threat or attack missed by the GenAI-based system and whether the organization had taken appropriate steps to assess and mitigate the risk of such threats based on available threat intelligence and security guidance.
- The comparative negligence or fault of other parties involved in the incident, such as the attackers themselves or any third-party vendors or partners whose actions or omissions may have contributed to the attack's success.

In cases where a false negative leads to a significant security breach or data loss, the organization using the GenAI-based system may face liability under various legal and regulatory frameworks, such as data protection laws, industry-specific regulations, or contractual obligations to customers or partners. Depending on the circumstances, this liability could result in financial penalties, legal damages, or reputational harm to the organization.

To mitigate the risks of liability for false positives and false negatives, organizations using GenAI-based systems for threat detection should take proactive steps such as:

- Ensuring the GenAI-based system is properly designed, tested, and validated for its intended use case and based on representative and unbiased training data.
- Implementing appropriate human oversight and control mechanisms, such as manual review processes or override capabilities, to allow for timely identification and correction of any errors or anomalies in the system's decisions.

- Maintaining detailed documentation and audit trails of the system's performance and decisions and any human interventions or adjustments made to the system over time.
- Regularly monitoring and assessing the system's performance metrics, such as precision, recall, and F1 scores, to identify any potential issues or areas for improvement.
- Engaging with legal and regulatory experts to ensure that the GenAI-based system complies with applicable laws and standards and that appropriate contractual protections and disclaimers are in place for any third-party vendors or users of the system.

By taking these steps, organizations can help to ensure that they are using GenAI-based systems for threat detection in a responsible and accountable manner and can minimize the risks of liability for any false positives or false negatives that may occur.

4.3.1.2 Accountability in Automated Incident Response

Another area where the question of responsibility and accountability arises is using GenAI for automated incident response. As GenAI-based systems become more sophisticated and autonomous, they may be able to take actions to contain and mitigate cyber threats without direct human intervention, such as isolating infected devices, blocking malicious traffic, or even launching counter-attacks against attackers.

While automated incident response can help reduce the time and effort required to respond to cyber incidents and minimize the potential impact of attacks, it also raises important questions about accountability and control. If a GenAI-based system takes inappropriate or excessive action in response to a perceived threat, such as shutting down a critical business system or deleting important data, who is responsible for the resulting damages or disruptions?

To ensure accountability in the use of GenAI for automated incident response, organizations should consider implementing several safeguards and controls, such as:

- Clearly defining the scope and parameters of the GenAI-based system's automated response capabilities, including the specific types of threats and incidents it is authorized to respond to and the specific actions it can take in each case.
- Implementing human-in-the-loop oversight mechanisms, such as manual approval processes or real-time monitoring and intervention capabilities, ensures that automated response actions are appropriate and proportional to the severity and urgency of the incident.
- Establishing clear escalation and notification protocols to ensure that human operators are promptly informed of any automated response actions taken by the GenAI-based system and can take manual control of the response process if necessary.
- Maintaining detailed logs and audit trails of all automated response actions taken by the GenAI-based system, including the specific threats and incidents that triggered each action, and the resulting outcomes and impacts of each action.
- Regularly test and validate the performance and effectiveness of the GenAI-based system's automated response capabilities, using simulated threat scenarios and incident response exercises, to identify potential issues or improvement areas.
- Ensuring that the GenAI-based system's automated response capabilities are aligned with the organization's overall incident response plan and procedures and that they are integrated with

other security tools and processes in a coordinated and consistent manner.

By implementing these safeguards and controls, organizations can help to ensure that the use of GenAI for automated incident response is accountable and transparent and that human operators remain in ultimate control of the response process. This can help minimize the risks of inappropriate or excessive actions being taken by the GenAI-based system and ensure that the organization remains responsible and liable for the outcomes of any automated response actions.

However, even with these safeguards in place, there may still be situations where using GenAI for automated incident response raises difficult questions of accountability and responsibility. For example, suppose a GenAI-based system takes a computerized response action that causes unintended harm or damage to the organization's systems, data, customers, or partners. In that case, who is ultimately liable for the resulting losses or legal claims may be unclear.

Similarly, suppose an attacker compromises or manipulates a GenAI-based system and uses it to launch automated response actions that harm third parties or violate laws or regulations. In that case, it may be difficult to determine whether the organization using the system, its developers, or the attackers are primarily responsible for the resulting damages or penalties.

To address these challenges, it may be necessary to develop new legal and regulatory frameworks specifically tailored to the use of AI in cybersecurity, which can provide clear guidance on liability, accountability, and responsibility issues in the context of automated incident response and other AI-based security functions. These frameworks may need to balance the benefits and risks of using AI for cybersecurity while ensuring that organizations and individuals are held accountable for the decisions and actions of their AI-based systems fairly and transparently.

4.3.2 Ethical guidelines for deploying GenAI in cybersecurity

In addition to the issues of accountability and responsibility, the use of GenAI in cybersecurity raises important ethical considerations. As these systems become more powerful and autonomous, ensuring they are being developed and deployed in a way consistent with human values and societal norms and do not cause unintended harm or perpetuate existing biases and inequalities is crucial.

To address these ethical challenges, it is important to establish clear guidelines and principles for the responsible development and deployment of GenAI in cybersecurity. These guidelines should be grounded in a human-centric approach that prioritizes the well-being and rights of individuals and society while recognizing the legitimate security objectives and interests of organizations and governments.

4.3.2.1 Principles of fairness, transparency, and human-centricity

One key principle for the ethical deployment of GenAI in cybersecurity is fairness. This means ensuring that the benefits and risks of these systems are distributed equitably across different groups and individuals and that they do not discriminate or disadvantage certain populations based on factors such as race, gender, age, or socioeconomic status.

To promote fairness in the use of GenAI for cybersecurity, organizations should take steps such as:

- Ensuring that the training data used to develop GenAI models is diverse, representative, and unbiased does not perpetuate historical or systemic inequalities.
- Implementing technical and procedural safeguards to detect and mitigate any biases or disparate impacts that may arise in GenAI-based systems, such as regular auditing and testing for fairness and non-discrimination.
- Engaging with diverse stakeholders and communities in developing and deploying GenAI-based systems ensures that their perspectives and concerns are considered and addressed.
- Providing clear and accessible information to individuals about how their data is being used by GenAI-based systems and what rights and protections they have under relevant laws and regulations.

Another key principle for the ethical deployment of GenAI in cybersecurity is transparency. This means ensuring these systems' decision-making processes and outcomes are explainable, auditable, and accountable to human oversight and control.

To promote transparency in the use of GenAI for cybersecurity, organizations should take steps such as:

- Developing and documenting clear policies and procedures for designing, testing, deploying, and monitoring GenAI-based systems, including the roles and responsibilities of stakeholders involved in these processes.
- Implementing technical measures to ensure that the inputs, out-

puts, and internal workings of GenAI models are traceable and interpretable, such as using explainable AI techniques or maintaining detailed logs and audit trails.
- Providing regular reports and disclosures to relevant stakeholders, such as customers, regulators, and the public, about the use and performance of GenAI-based systems, including any incidents or issues that may arise.
- Enabling human oversight and intervention in the operation of GenAI-based systems through manual review processes, override capabilities, or real-time monitoring and control interfaces.

Human-centricity is a third key principle for the ethical deployment of GenAI in cybersecurity. This means ensuring that these systems are designed and used to respect and promote human agency, autonomy, and dignity and not undermine or replace human judgment and decision-making.

To promote human-centricity in the use of GenAI for cybersecurity, organizations should take steps such as:

- Involving human operators and domain experts in designing, testing, and deploying GenAI-based systems to ensure they align with human values, norms, and expectations.
- Providing clear and meaningful opportunities for human oversight, control, and redress in GenAI-based systems, such as manual review processes, appeals mechanisms, or user feedback channels.
- Ensuring that GenAI-based systems augment and support human decision-making rather than replace or automate it entirely and that human actors remain ultimately responsible and accountable for the outcomes of these systems.

- Promoting public awareness, dialogue, and participation in the development and governance of GenAI-based systems to ensure they are responsive to societal needs and concerns and earn and maintain public trust and legitimacy.

By adhering to these principles of fairness, transparency, and human-centricity, organizations can help to ensure that the deployment of GenAI in cybersecurity is ethical, responsible, and aligned with human values and interests. However, implementing these principles in practice may require significant changes to existing organizational cultures, processes, incentives, and ongoing collaboration and dialogue among stakeholders and disciplines.

4.3.2.2 Balancing security objectives with individual privacy rights

One ethical challenge in using GenAI for cybersecurity is balancing legitimate security objectives with individual privacy rights and civil liberties. While AI and machine learning techniques can help detect and prevent cyber threats more effectively and efficiently, they can also enable more invasive and intrusive surveillance, profiling, and behavioral analysis forms.

For example, a GenAI-based system designed to detect insider threats within an organization may be able to analyze a wide range of data sources, such as email communications, social media activity, and biometric information, to identify patterns or anomalies that may indicate malicious intent or behavior. While this type of analysis may be justified from a security perspective, it can also raise significant privacy concerns, particularly if the data is collected or used without the knowledge or consent of the individuals involved.

Similarly, a GenAI-based system used for threat intelligence gathering or attribution may combine and analyze data from multiple sources, such as network traffic logs, dark web forums, and public records, to identify the actors or groups behind specific cyber attacks or campaigns. While this type of analysis can be valuable for deterrence and response efforts, it can also enable more targeted and invasive forms of surveillance and profiling, which may disproportionately impact certain communities or populations.

To balance these competing objectives and ensure that the use of GenAI in cybersecurity is consistent with individual privacy rights and civil liberties, organizations should consider implementing several ethical safeguards and principles, such as:

- Adhering to relevant laws, regulations, and data protection and privacy standards, such as the European Union's General Data Protection Regulation (GDPR) or the California Consumer Privacy Act (CCPA), which set out specific requirements for collecting, using, and sharing personal data.
- Implementing data minimization and purpose limitation principles requires that only the minimum amount necessary for a specific security purpose be collected and used and that the data not be repurposed or shared for other unrelated purposes without explicit consent.
- Providing clear and transparent notice to individuals about the types of data being collected and analyzed by GenAI-based systems, the purposes for which the data is being used, and the safeguards in place to protect their privacy and rights.
- Enabling individual control and choice over the collection and use of their data through mechanisms such as opt-in consent, data portability, or the right to be forgotten allows individuals to exercise

greater autonomy and agency over their personal information.
- Implementing technical and organizational measures to secure and protect the data used by GenAI-based systems, such as encryption, access controls, or data segregation, prevents unauthorized access, use, or disclosure of personal information.
- Conducting regular privacy impact assessments and audits of GenAI-based systems to identify and mitigate any risks or harms to individual privacy and civil liberties and to ensure compliance with relevant laws and regulations.
- Engaging with privacy advocates, civil society groups, and other stakeholders in developing and deploying GenAI-based systems ensures that their concerns and perspectives are considered and addressed in the design and operation of these systems.

By implementing these ethical safeguards and principles, organizations can help to ensure that the use of GenAI in cybersecurity is consistent with individual privacy rights and civil liberties and that it does not enable or perpetuate forms of surveillance or profiling that are disproportionate, discriminatory, or harmful to certain individuals or groups.

However, balancing security objectives with privacy rights is not always straightforward and may require difficult trade-offs and compromises in specific contexts or situations. For example, in the case of a significant or imminent cyber threat, an organization may need to collect or analyze more extensive or sensitive data to detect and prevent the attack, even if this data collection may raise privacy concerns in other contexts.

Similarly, in the case of a criminal investigation or national security matter, law enforcement or intelligence agencies may need to access or use data collected by GenAI-based systems in ways that may be justified under relevant legal authorities but that may also raise concerns about the scope and intrusiveness of government surveillance powers.

To navigate these complex trade-offs and ensure that the use of GenAI in cybersecurity remains ethical and accountable, it is important to have clear and transparent decision-making and oversight processes involving multiple stakeholders and perspectives guided by a shared set of values and principles. This may require ongoing dialogue and collaboration among technologists, policymakers, civil society groups, and the public to develop and refine ethical frameworks and guidelines that can help balance security objectives with individual privacy rights fairly and proportionally.

Ultimately, the ethical deployment of GenAI in cybersecurity requires a commitment to human-centric values and principles, prioritizing the well-being and dignity of individuals and society while recognizing the legitimate security interests and objectives of organizations and governments. By adhering to these values and principles and engaging in ongoing reflection and dialogue about the ethical implications of these powerful new technologies, we can help ensure that the benefits of GenAI in cybersecurity are realized in a way consistent with our shared human values and aspirations.

5. Addressing the Challenges of GenAI in Cybersecurity

As explored in the previous sections, using GenAI in cybersecurity presents significant opportunities and challenges. While these powerful new technologies can help detect and prevent cyber threats more effectively and efficiently, they raise important concerns about bias, transparency, accountability, and ethics. To realize the full potential of GenAI in cybersecurity, it is essential to develop and implement strategies and techniques for addressing these challenges proactively and systematically.

In this section, we will focus specifically on the challenge of bias in GenAI models and explore a range of techniques and approaches for mitigating and managing this bias in cybersecurity applications. We will discuss the importance of diverse and representative training data, the use of fairness-aware model architectures and optimization techniques, and the need for continuous monitoring and auditing of GenAI models for bias throughout their lifecycle.

5. ADDRESSING THE CHALLENGES OF GENAI IN CYBERSECURITY

5.1 Techniques for Mitigating Bias in GenAI Models

Biases in GenAI models can arise from various sources, including biases in the training data, biases in the model architecture or optimization process, and biases in how the model is used or interpreted in practice. To mitigate these biases and ensure that GenAI models are fair, equitable, and trustworthy, it is important to adopt a multifaceted approach that addresses bias at each model development and deployment stage.

5.1.1 Diverse and representative training data

One of the most important techniques for mitigating bias in GenAI models is to ensure that the training data used to develop these models is diverse, representative, and unbiased. This means carefully selecting and curating the data sources and samples used to train the model to ensure they reflect the full range of perspectives, experiences, and outcomes relevant to cybersecurity.

For example, when training a GenAI model to detect and classify cyber threats, it is important to include data from a wide variety of sources and contexts, such as different types of networks, devices, and applications, as well as other geographic regions, industry sectors, and user populations. This can help ensure that the model is not overly biased towards certain threats or environments and can generalize effectively to new and unseen scenarios.

Similarly, when training a GenAI model to identify and respond to security incidents, it is important to include data from a diverse range of past incidents and response actions to ensure that the model is not biased toward certain incidents or response strategies. This may require actively seeking out and incorporating data from underrepresented or marginalized groups, such as small businesses, nonprofit organizations, or minority communities, to ensure that their experiences and perspectives are adequately reflected in the model.

To ensure the diversity and representativeness of training data, organizations can take several steps, such as:

- Conducting data audits and assessments to identify and measure any biases or limitations in existing data sources and samples and to develop strategies for addressing these biases through data augmentation, resampling, or other techniques.
- Collaborating with diverse stakeholders and domain experts, such as security researchers, incident responders, and community representatives, to identify and incorporate relevant data sources and perspectives that may be missing or underrepresented in current datasets.
- Implementing data governance and management policies and practices that prioritize diversity, inclusion, and equity in the collection, curation, and use of training data and establishing clear roles and responsibilities for ensuring data quality and integrity.
- Providing training and resources to data scientists, engineers, and other staff involved in developing GenAI models, raising awareness of bias and fairness issues, and equipping them with the skills and tools needed to identify and mitigate bias in their work.

By prioritizing the diversity and representativeness of training data, organizations can help ensure that their GenAI models are built on a

5. ADDRESSING THE CHALLENGES OF GENAI IN CYBERSECURITY

solid and unbiased foundation and perform accurately and equitably across a wide range of scenarios and populations.

5.1.2 Fairness-aware model architectures and optimization

In addition to ensuring the diversity and representativeness of training data, another important technique for mitigating bias in GenAI models is to use fairness-aware model architectures and optimization techniques. These approaches aim to explicitly incorporate considerations of fairness and non-discrimination into the design and training of GenAI models to ensure that they can perform equitably and avoid perpetuating or amplifying existing biases.

One example of a fairness-aware model architecture is adversarial debiasing techniques, which aim to remove or minimize discriminatory correlations or patterns in the model's outputs or decisions. These techniques typically involve training a separate adversarial network alongside the main GenAI model, which tries to predict sensitive attributes (such as race, gender, or age) based on the model's outputs. By penalizing the model for any ability to predict these sensitive attributes, the adversarial network can help remove discriminatory information from the model's decisions while preserving its overall accuracy and performance.

Another example of a fairness-aware optimization technique is constraint-based optimization, which explicitly incorporates fairness constraints or objectives into the model training process. For example, a GenAI model for detecting insider threats could be trained with a constraint requiring the model to have similar false positive rates across different demographic groups to ensure that it does not disproportionately flag certain individuals or communities as potential threats. Similarly, a GenAI model for recommending security controls could be trained with an objective that prioritizes the equitable distribution of security benefits and costs across different user populations or business units.

To implement fairness-aware model architectures and optimization techniques, organizations can take several steps, such as:

- Collaborating with domain experts and stakeholders to identify and prioritize the specific fairness criteria and objectives relevant to cybersecurity, such as equal false positive rates, demographic parity, or individual fairness.
- Experimenting with different fairness-aware model architectures and optimization techniques, such as adversarial debiasing, constraint-based optimization, or multi-objective optimization, to identify the approaches that are most effective and appropriate for the specific use case and data.
- Incorporating fairness metrics and evaluation procedures into the model development and testing process to assess and compare the performance and fairness of different model variants and configurations and to select the most equitable and effective models for deployment.
- Providing training and resources to data scientists, engineers, and other staff involved in developing GenAI models to build their knowledge and skills in fairness-aware modeling techniques and to empower them to identify and address potential bias issues in their work.

By using fairness-aware model architectures and optimization techniques, organizations can help ensure that their GenAI models are designed and trained to explicitly consider and mitigate potential biases and disparities, promoting more equitable and trustworthy outcomes in the context of cybersecurity applications.

5.1.3 Continuous monitoring and auditing for bias

While using diverse and representative training data, fairness-aware model architectures, and optimization techniques can help mitigate bias in GenAI models at the development stage, it is also important to recognize that bias can emerge or evolve as the models are deployed and used in real-world contexts. To address this challenge, it is essential to implement continuous monitoring and auditing processes to detect and assess bias in GenAI models throughout their lifecycle and enable timely and effective interventions to mitigate any identified biases.

Continuous monitoring and auditing for bias in GenAI models can involve a range of activities and techniques, such as:

- Regularly testing and evaluating the performance and fairness of deployed GenAI models using real-world data and scenarios to identify deviations or disparities from expected or desired outcomes and assess the impact and severity of any identified biases.
- Conduct periodic audits and assessments of the data pipelines, model architectures, and decision processes used in deployed GenAI models to identify any sources of bias or unfairness that may have been introduced or amplified over time and to develop strategies for addressing these issues.

- Engaging with diverse stakeholders and communities, such as security practitioners, end-users, and advocacy groups, to solicit feedback and input on the performance and fairness of deployed GenAI models and to identify any concerns or issues that may not be visible through internal monitoring and auditing processes.
- Implementing mechanisms for transparency and accountability in using GenAI models, such as providing clear and accessible information to users about how the models work and how their data is being used and establishing channels for users to report any concerns or complaints about bias or unfairness.
- Developing and implementing policies and procedures for responding to identified biases or unfairness in deployed GenAI models, such as retraining or updating the models with new data or architectures, adjusting decision thresholds or outputs, or providing additional human oversight or intervention.

To operationalize continuous monitoring and auditing for bias in GenAI models, organizations can take several steps, such as:

- Establishing dedicated teams or roles responsible for monitoring and auditing the performance and fairness of deployed GenAI models, with clear mandates, resources, and accountability mechanisms.
- Developing and implementing standardized metrics, frameworks, and tools for measuring and assessing bias and fairness in GenAI models, drawing on best practices and guidance from academia, industry, and civil society.
- Investing in data infrastructure and management processes that enable efficient and secure collection, storage, and analysis of real-world data for monitoring and auditing purposes while protecting

user privacy and security.
- Providing training and resources to staff involved in monitoring and auditing GenAI models to build their knowledge and skills in bias detection and mitigation techniques and to empower them to proactively and promptly identify and address potential bias issues.
- Collaborating with external stakeholders and experts, such as academic researchers, industry partners, and advocacy groups, to share knowledge and best practices, validate and improve monitoring and auditing processes, and build public trust and confidence in using GenAI models.

By implementing continuous monitoring and auditing processes for bias in GenAI models, organizations can help ensure that these models remain fair, equitable, and trustworthy over time and that any emerging biases or disparities are quickly identified and addressed. This can help promote more effective and ethical use of GenAI in cybersecurity and build greater public trust and confidence in these powerful new technologies.

5.2 Approaches to Improving Explainability and Interpretability

As discussed in the previous sections, one key challenge in using GenAI for cybersecurity is the lack of explainability and interpretability in many of these models. The complex and opaque nature of deep learning algorithms can make it difficult for human users to understand how these models arrive at their decisions or predictions, which can limit their usefulness and trustworthiness in high-stakes cybersecurity contexts.

To address this challenge, researchers and practitioners have developed a range of approaches and techniques for improving the explainability and interpretability of GenAI models. These approaches can be broadly categorized into three main areas: developing inherently interpretable GenAI models, providing post-hoc explanations and visualizations, and incorporating human-in-the-loop approaches for interpretability.

5.2.1 Developing inherently interpretable GenAI models

One approach to improving the explainability and interpretability of GenAI models is to develop inherently interpretable models by design. This means using model architectures, training techniques, and feature representations that are more transparent and understandable to human users rather than relying on complex and opaque deep learning algorithms.

Some examples of inherently interpretable GenAI models that have been explored in the context of cybersecurity include:

- **Rule-based models:** These models use a set of explicit, human-readable rules to make decisions or predictions based on input features. For example, a rule-based model for detecting phishing emails might use regulations such as "IF the email contains a suspicious URL AND the sender is not in the user's contact list, THEN classify the email as phishing." While rule-based models may not be as powerful or flexible as deep learning models, they are often more interpretable and easier to validate and debug.

5. ADDRESSING THE CHALLENGES OF GENAI IN CYBERSECURITY

- **Decision trees and random forests:** These models use a hierarchical tree structure to make decisions based on binary splits on input features. Each node in the tree represents a decision point, and the path from the root to a leaf node represents a specific combination of feature values that leads to a particular output or prediction. Decision trees and random forests are often more interpretable than deep learning models, as the decision logic can be visualized and traced back to specific input features.
- **Linear models:** These models use a linear combination of input features to make predictions or decisions, with each feature being assigned a weight that reflects its importance or contribution to the output. Linear models, such as logistic regression or support vector machines, are often more interpretable than deep learning models, as the weights can be directly inspected and interpreted in terms of the original input features.
- **Bayesian models:** These models use probabilistic graphical models to represent the relationships and dependencies between input features and output variables and to make decisions or predictions based on Bayesian inference. Bayesian models, such as Bayesian networks or Markov models, are often more interpretable than deep learning models, as the model structure and parameters can be directly inspected and interpreted in terms of domain knowledge and assumptions.

To develop inherently interpretable GenAI models for cybersecurity, organizations can take several steps, such as:

- Collaborating with domain experts and stakeholders to identify the key features, relationships, and decision criteria relevant to the specific cybersecurity task or application and formulate these into

explicit rules, trees, or probabilistic models.
- Experimenting with different inherently interpretable model architectures and training techniques and comparing their performance and interpretability to deep learning models to identify the approaches that offer the best balance of accuracy and transparency for the specific use case.
- Incorporating interpretability metrics and evaluation procedures into the model development and testing process to assess and compare the explainability and understandability of different model variants and configurations and to select the most interpretable models for deployment.
- Providing training and resources to data scientists, engineers, and other staff involved in developing GenAI models to build their knowledge and skills in inherently interpretable modeling techniques and to empower them to create more transparent and understandable models for cybersecurity applications.

By developing inherently interpretable GenAI models for cybersecurity, organizations can help to improve the transparency, trust, and accountability of these powerful new technologies and enable more effective collaboration and communication between human users and AI systems.

5.2.2 Post-hoc explanations and visualizations

While inherently interpretable GenAI models can offer significant benefits in transparency and understandability, they may not always be feasible or desirable in all cybersecurity contexts. In some cases, the complexity and richness of the data and decision spaces may require more powerful and flexible deep learning models, which can be more difficult to interpret directly.

In these cases, another approach to improving the explainability and interpretability of GenAI models is to provide post-hoc explanations and visualizations that help to illuminate the decision-making process and outputs of these models. Post-hoc explanations are generated after the model has made a decision or prediction and aim to provide human-understandable insights into the key factors, features, or relationships that influenced the model's output.

Some examples of post-hoc explanation techniques that have been explored in the context of GenAI for cybersecurity include:

- **Feature importance and attribution:** These techniques aim to quantify the contribution or importance of each input feature to the model's output and to visualize these contributions in a way that is understandable to human users. Common feature techniques include permutation importance, SHAP (SHapley Additive exPlanations), and LIME (Local Interpretable Model-agnostic Explanations), which can highlight the most influential features for a particular decision or prediction.
- **Saliency maps and attention mechanisms:** These techniques aim to visualize the regions or elements of the input data that the model focuses on or attends to when making a decision or prediction. For example, a saliency map for an image classification model might highlight the pixels or regions most important for identifying a particular object or class, while an attention mechanism for a natural language processing model might underline the words or phrases most relevant for answering a specific question.

- **Counterfactual explanations:** These techniques aim to generate alternative scenarios or examples that show how the model's output would change if certain input features or conditions were different. For example, a counterfactual explanation for a malware detection model might show that if a particular API call or file access pattern were removed from the input, the model would no longer classify the sample as malicious. Counterfactual explanations can help identify the key factors that drive the model's decisions and explore the model's robustness and sensitivity to different input variations.
- **Rule extraction and decision trees:** These techniques aim to extract human-readable rules or decision trees from a trained deep learning model, which can provide a more interpretable and transparent representation of the model's decision logic. Rule extraction techniques, such as CRED (Contrastive Rule Extraction via Decision Trees) or REFNE (Rule Extraction From Neural Networks Ensemble), can generate if-then rules that approximate the model's behavior. In contrast, decision tree techniques, such as TREPAN (TREes PArroting Networks), can create decision trees that mimic the model's outputs.

To provide post-hoc explanations and visualizations for GenAI models in cybersecurity, organizations can take several steps, such as:

- Experimenting with different post-hoc explanation techniques and tools and comparing their effectiveness and usability for various types of GenAI models and cybersecurity tasks to identify the approaches that offer the most informative and actionable insights for human users.
- Incorporating explanation and visualization capabilities into the GenAI model development and deployment workflows to enable

5. ADDRESSING THE CHALLENGES OF GENAI IN CYBERSECURITY

the automated generation and delivery of post-hoc explanations and visualizations to human users in real-time or near-real-time.
- Providing training and resources to cybersecurity analysts, incident responders, and other staff using the GenAI models and explanations to build their knowledge and skills in interpreting and acting on these tools' insights and enable more effective human-AI collaboration and decision-making.
- Conducting user studies and gathering feedback from human users on the clarity, usefulness, and trustworthiness of the post-hoc explanations and visualizations and using this feedback to improve and refine the explanation techniques and interfaces iteratively.
- Establishing guidelines and best practices for generating and using post-hoc explanations and visualizations in cybersecurity contexts to ensure that these tools are used responsibly, transparently, and accountable and to mitigate any potential risks or unintended consequences.

By providing post-hoc explanations and visualizations for GenAI models in cybersecurity, organizations can help bridge the gap between the complexity and opacity of these models and the need for human understanding and trust in their decisions and actions. This can enable more effective and informed use of GenAI in cybersecurity and help build public confidence and acceptance of these powerful new technologies.

5.2.3 Human-in-the-loop approaches for interpretability

While inherently interpretable models and post-hoc explanations can help improve the transparency and understandability of GenAI models in cybersecurity, they may not always be sufficient to ensure that human users can effectively interpret and act on these models' insights. In some cases, the complexity and uncertainty of the cybersecurity domain may require more active and collaborative involvement of human experts in the decision-making process to provide additional context, judgment, and oversight.

To address this challenge, researchers and practitioners have explored various human-in-the-loop approaches for enhancing the interpretability and trustworthiness of GenAI models in cybersecurity. These approaches aim to create more interactive and collaborative workflows between human users and AI systems, where the human can provide input, feedback, and guidance to the model, and the model can adapt and improve its performance based on this human input.

Some examples of human-in-the-loop approaches for GenAI interpretability in cybersecurity include:

- **Interactive machine learning:** This approach involves creating interactive interfaces and tools that allow human users to actively participate in model development and training by providing labeled examples, feature selections, or other forms of domain knowledge and expertise. For example, a cybersecurity analyst might use an interactive machine learning tool to label network traffic data as benign or malicious and select the most informative features for detecting different types of threats. The GenAI model can then learn from this human input and adapt its decision boundaries and feature weights accordingly, creating a more accurate and interpretable model that reflects the human's domain knowledge and intuition.
- **Collaborative decision-making:** This approach involves creating

5. ADDRESSING THE CHALLENGES OF GENAI IN CYBERSECURITY

collaborative interfaces and workflows that allow human users to work alongside GenAI models in real-time decision-making tasks, such as incident triage, threat hunting, or response planning. For example, a cybersecurity incident response team might use a collaborative decision-making tool that combines the outputs of multiple GenAI models (e.g., anomaly detection, malware classification, threat intelligence) with the expertise and judgment of human analysts to identify and prioritize the most critical and actionable security events. The human analysts can provide additional context and reasoning for their decisions. They can override or adjust the model's recommendations based on their experience and intuition. In contrast, the GenAI models can provide rapid and scalable analysis of large volumes of data and can highlight potential blind spots or biases in the human decision-making process.

- **Explainable query and feedback:** This approach involves creating query and feedback interfaces that allow human users to ask questions and provide input to GenAI models to understand better and interpret their decisions and outputs. For example, a cybersecurity analyst might use an explainable query interface to ask a GenAI model why it flagged a particular network connection as suspicious or what additional evidence it would need to classify it as benign. The GenAI model can generate human-understandable explanations or visualizations highlighting the key features or patterns influencing its decision. It can also suggest alternative scenarios or counterfactuals that could change its output. The human analyst can then provide feedback on the quality and usefulness of these explanations and can suggest additional factors or contexts that the model should consider in its analysis.
- **Iterative refinement and adaptation:** This approach involves creating iterative workflows and feedback loops that allow human users to continuously refine and adapt GenAI models based on

their real-world performance and outcomes. For example, a cybersecurity operations team might deploy a GenAI model to detect and respond to phishing attacks and monitor its performance and effectiveness over time. If the model generates too many false positives or false negatives, or if it fails to adapt to new types of phishing tactics, the human team can provide feedback and additional training data to the model. It can work with the model developers to adjust its architecture, parameters, or decision thresholds. This iterative refinement process can help to create a more robust and interpretable model that evolves and improves based on real-world experience and human expertise.

To implement human-in-the-loop approaches for GenAI interpretability in cybersecurity, organizations can take several steps, such as:

- Conducting user research and needs assessments to understand the challenges and requirements for human-AI collaboration and interpretability in different cybersecurity roles and workflows and identify the most promising opportunities for human-in-the-loop approaches.
- Developing and testing different human-in-the-loop interfaces, tools, and workflows for GenAI models in cybersecurity and evaluating their usability, effectiveness, and impact on human decision-making and performance.
- Providing training and resources to cybersecurity staff on effectively collaborating with and interpreting GenAI models using human-in-the-loop approaches and establishing clear roles, responsibilities, and communication channels for human-AI teams.
- Establishing governance and accountability frameworks for human-in-the-loop GenAI models in cybersecurity, including policies

and procedures for human oversight, testing and validation of model outputs, and documenting and auditing human-AI decision-making processes.
- Continuously monitoring and evaluating the performance and outcomes of human-in-the-loop GenAI models in real-world cybersecurity contexts and using this feedback to improve and adapt the models and workflows over time iteratively.

By adopting human-in-the-loop approaches for GenAI interpretability in cybersecurity, organizations can create more transparent, accountable, and effective AI systems that leverage the complementary strengths of human and machine intelligence. This can help build greater trust and adoption of GenAI in cybersecurity and enable more agile and resilient defenses against evolving cyber threats.

5.3 Establishing Accountability Frameworks and Ethical Guidelines

As GenAI systems become increasingly integrated into cybersecurity workflows and decision-making processes, it is crucial to establish clear accountability frameworks and ethical guidelines to ensure their responsible and trustworthy deployment. Without such frameworks and guidelines, there is a risk that GenAI systems could be misused, abused, or deployed in ways that violate human rights, privacy, or other fundamental values.

Accountability frameworks refer to the policies, procedures, and mechanisms implemented to ensure that the developers, operators, and users of GenAI systems are held responsible for their actions and decisions and that there are clear channels for redress and remediation when things go wrong. On the other hand, ethical guidelines refer to the principles and values that should guide the design, development, and deployment of GenAI systems to ensure that they are aligned with societal norms and expectations and promote the well-being and flourishing of individuals and communities.

This section will explore key considerations and approaches for establishing accountability frameworks and ethical guidelines for GenAI in cybersecurity, including defining roles and responsibilities, developing industry standards and best practices, engaging with stakeholders, and incorporating societal values.

5.3.1 Defining roles and responsibilities for GenAI deployment

One of the first steps in establishing accountability frameworks for GenAI in cybersecurity is clearly defining the roles and responsibilities of the various stakeholders involved in developing, deploying, and using these systems. This includes:

- **GenAI developers and researchers:** These individuals and teams are responsible for designing, building, and testing GenAI models and algorithms for cybersecurity applications. They should be accountable for ensuring that their models are accurate, reliable, and unbiased and that they are developed using ethical and accountable AI practices, such as data privacy, security, and fairness. They should also be responsible for providing clear documentation and explanations of how their models work and collaborating with other stakeholders to ensure their effective and responsible deployment.

- **Cybersecurity operators and analysts:** These individuals and teams are responsible for deploying and using GenAI systems in cybersecurity workflows and decision-making processes. They should ensure they have the necessary skills, knowledge, and training to operate and interpret GenAI systems effectively and use them per established policies, procedures, and ethical guidelines. They should also be responsible for monitoring the performance and outcomes of GenAI systems and providing feedback and input to developers and other stakeholders to improve and adapt these systems continuously.

- **Organizational leaders and decision-makers:** These are the individuals and teams responsible for setting the strategic direction and priorities for cybersecurity within their organizations and making decisions about adopting and deploying GenAI systems. They should be responsible for ensuring that GenAI systems are aligned with organizational goals and values and deployed in a way that is transparent, accountable, and respectful of stakeholder concerns and expectations. They should also be responsible for allocating the necessary resources and support for the effective and responsible deployment of GenAI systems and for establishing clear governance and oversight mechanisms to ensure ongoing compliance and performance.

- **Legal and regulatory authorities:** These individuals and teams are responsible for setting and enforcing legal and regulatory frameworks for using AI and other emerging technologies in cybersecurity and other domains. They should ensure that GenAI systems are developed and deployed in compliance with relevant laws, regulations, and ethical standards and provide clear guidance and oversight to organizations and individuals involved in their development and use. They should also be responsible for investigating and prosecuting cases of misuse or abuse of GenAI systems and providing remedies and redress to individuals or groups whom these systems have harmed.

To effectively define and implement these roles and responsibilities, organizations and stakeholders involved in the development and deployment of GenAI systems in cybersecurity should:

- Develop clear and comprehensive policies and procedures that outline each stakeholder group's expectations, obligations, and liabilities. That guide handles different scenarios and challenges when developing and deploying GenAI systems.
- Establish clear lines of communication and collaboration between different stakeholder groups to ensure that everyone is working towards common goals and values and that there is a shared understanding of the risks and benefits of GenAI systems in cybersecurity.
- Provide regular training and education to all stakeholders on the technical, operational, legal, and ethical aspects of GenAI cybersecurity systems. This ensures everyone has the necessary knowledge and skills to effectively and responsibly perform their roles and responsibilities.
- Implement robust monitoring and auditing mechanisms to track the performance and outcomes of GenAI systems in real-world deployments and to identify and address any issues or concerns that may arise over time.
- Establish clear accountability and liability frameworks that hold stakeholders responsible for their actions and decisions related to GenAI systems and that provide clear channels for reporting and addressing any violations or harms that may occur.

By clearly defining and implementing these roles and responsibilities, organizations and stakeholders can create a more transparent, accountable, and trustworthy ecosystem for developing and deploying GenAI systems in cybersecurity. They can help to ensure that these systems are used in ways that promote the public good and respect individual rights and freedoms.

5.3.2 Developing industry standards and best practices

Another key element of establishing accountability frameworks and ethical guidelines for GenAI in cybersecurity is developing industry standards and best practices. These agreed-upon norms, principles, and procedures should guide the development, testing, deployment, and monitoring of GenAI systems across different organizations and domains.

Industry standards and best practices can help create a level playing field for the responsible development and use of GenAI systems by providing a common set of expectations and requirements that all stakeholders should adhere to. They can also help promote transparency, consistency, and interoperability between different GenAI systems and workflows and facilitate sharing knowledge and resources between various organizations and communities.

Some examples of industry standards and best practices that are relevant to GenAI in cybersecurity include:

- **Ethical AI frameworks:** These are the high-level principles and values that should guide the development and use of AI systems in general and GenAI systems in particular. Some widely recognized ethical AI frameworks include the IEEE Global Initiative on Ethics of Autonomous and Intelligent Systems, the OECD Principles on AI, and the EU Ethics Guidelines for Trustworthy AI. These frameworks typically emphasize principles such as transparency, accountability, fairness, privacy, security, and human-centricity and guide operationalizing these principles in practice.

- **Data governance standards:** These are the policies and procedures that should be followed to ensure the responsible and secure collection, storage, use, and sharing of data for GenAI systems in cybersecurity. Some relevant data governance standards include the NIST Privacy Framework, the ISO/IEC 27001 standard for information security management, and the EU General Data Protection Regulation (GDPR). These standards typically cover issues such as data quality, data minimization, data protection, data rights, and data accountability and guide on implementing these practices in different organizational and technical contexts.
- **Model development and testing standards:** These are the methodologies and criteria that should be used to design, train, validate, and test GenAI models for cybersecurity applications. Some relevant model development and testing standards include the NIST AI Risk Management Framework, the IEEE P7001 standard for transparency of autonomous systems, and the ISO/IEC TR 24028 standard for trustworthiness in AI systems. These standards typically cover issues such as model architecture, training data, performance metrics, explainability, robustness, and fairness and guide evaluating and improving these aspects of GenAI models.
- **Deployment and monitoring standards:** These procedures and mechanisms should be used to deploy, operate, and monitor GenAI systems in real-world cybersecurity environments. Some relevant deployment and monitoring standards include the NIST SP 800-

5. ADDRESSING THE CHALLENGES OF GENAI IN CYBERSECURITY

160 standard for systems security engineering, the ISO/IEC 27032 standard for cybersecurity, and the MITRE ATT&CK framework for adversarial tactics and techniques. These standards typically cover issues such as system integration, configuration management, incident response, performance monitoring, and continuous improvement and guide ensuring the ongoing effectiveness and security of GenAI systems.

To develop and implement these industry standards and best practices, organizations and stakeholders involved in the development and deployment of GenAI systems in cybersecurity should:

- Actively participate in relevant standards development organizations and initiatives, such as the IEEE, ISO, NIST, and OECD, to contribute their expertise and perspectives and to help shape the direction and content of emerging standards and guidelines.
- Collaborate with other organizations and stakeholders to share knowledge, experiences, and resources related to developing and deploying GenAI systems in cybersecurity and identify common challenges and opportunities for standardization and best practice sharing.
- Adapt and customize existing standards and best practices to their organizations' and domains' specific needs and contexts while aligning with the broader ecosystem of GenAI systems and stakeholders.
- Provide training and support to their staff and partners on implementing and complying with relevant standards and best practices and establish clear mechanisms for monitoring and enforcing compliance over time.
- Continuously review and update their standards and best practices

based on new research, technologies, and experiences, and engage in ongoing dialogue and collaboration with other stakeholders to ensure these frameworks' continued relevance and effectiveness.

By developing and implementing robust industry standards and best practices for GenAI in cybersecurity, organizations, and stakeholders can help create a more consistent, reliable, and trustworthy ecosystem for the responsible development and deployment of these systems and mitigate the risks and challenges associated with their use in real-world environments.

5.3.3 Engaging with stakeholders and incorporating societal values

A third critical element of establishing accountability frameworks and ethical guidelines for GenAI in cybersecurity is engaging with stakeholders and incorporating societal values. This involves actively seeking out and considering the perspectives, concerns, and expectations of the various individuals, groups, and communities affected by or interested in developing and deploying GenAI systems in cybersecurity.

Stakeholder engagement is important because it helps to ensure that the accountability frameworks and ethical guidelines for GenAI are responsive to the needs and values of the broader society and are not just driven by the interests and priorities of the developers and deployers of these systems. It also helps to build trust, legitimacy, and support for GenAI systems among the public and other key stakeholders by demonstrating a commitment to transparency, inclusivity, and

5. ADDRESSING THE CHALLENGES OF GENAI IN CYBERSECURITY

responsiveness.

Some examples of key stakeholders that should be engaged in the development of accountability frameworks and ethical guidelines for GenAI in cybersecurity include:

- **Consumers and end-users:** These are the individuals and groups who are directly affected by the use of GenAI systems in cybersecurity, such as employees, customers, and citizens. They may have concerns about privacy, security, fairness, and transparency and may expect GenAI systems to be designed and deployed in ways that respect their rights and interests.
- **Civil society organizations:** These are the advocacy groups, think tanks, and other non-governmental organizations that represent the interests and values of different communities and constituencies. They may have expertise and insights on human rights, social justice, and environmental sustainability issues. They may expect GenAI systems to be developed and deployed in ways that promote these values.
- **Academic and research institutions:** These are the universities, research centers, and other educational institutions involved in studying and developing GenAI technologies and their societal implications. They may have expertise and insights on ethics, governance, and policy issues. They may expect GenAI systems to be developed and deployed in ways that are consistent with scientific and academic standards of rigor, objectivity, and integrity.
- **Industry associations and standards bodies:** These professional organizations and consortia represent the interests and practices of different industries and domains involved in developing and deploying GenAI systems. They may have expertise and insights on technical standards, best practices, and market trends. They

may expect GenAI systems to be developed and deployed in ways consistent with industry norms and expectations.
- **Policymakers and regulators:** These are the government officials and agencies responsible for setting and enforcing laws, regulations, and policies related to developing and deploying GenAI systems. They may have expertise and insights on public safety, national security, and economic competitiveness. They may expect GenAI systems to be developed and deployed in ways consistent with legal and regulatory requirements.

To effectively engage with these and other stakeholders, organizations, and individuals involved in the development and deployment of GenAI systems in cybersecurity, should:

- Conduct stakeholder mapping and analysis to identify the key stakeholders and their interests, concerns, and expectations related to GenAI systems in cybersecurity.
- Establish clear and accessible channels for communication and consultation with stakeholders, such as public forums, surveys, focus groups, and advisory boards, to gather input and feedback on the development and deployment of GenAI systems.
- Provide clear and transparent information to stakeholders about the goals, methods, and outcomes of GenAI systems in cybersecurity, and be responsive to their questions and concerns.
- Incorporate stakeholder input and feedback into the design, development, and deployment of GenAI systems, and be willing to make changes and adjustments based on this input.
- Establish clear mechanisms for stakeholder oversight and accountability, such as independent audits, impact assessments, and grievance procedures, to ensure that GenAI systems are being de-

veloped and deployed in ways that are consistent with stakeholder expectations and societal values.

By engaging with stakeholders and incorporating societal values into the development of accountability frameworks and ethical guidelines for GenAI in cybersecurity, organizations, and individuals can help ensure that these systems are developed and deployed in responsible, trustworthy, and beneficial ways to society as a whole. This can help build public trust and support for GenAI technologies and ensure they are used to promote the greater good while minimizing risks and harms.

5.4 Collaboration Between AI Researchers, Cybersecurity Experts, and Policymakers

Addressing the challenges and realizing the full potential of GenAI in cybersecurity requires close collaboration between AI researchers, cybersecurity experts, and policymakers. Each of these groups brings unique perspectives, knowledge, and skills to the table, and by working together, they can help ensure that GenAI systems are developed and deployed effectively, responsibly, and aligned with societal values and interests.

AI researchers are experts in the technical aspects of GenAI, including the design, development, and testing of GenAI models and algorithms. They have deep knowledge of the capabilities and limitations of different GenAI approaches and can provide insights on optimizing these approaches for different cybersecurity use cases and contexts.

Cybersecurity experts, on the other hand, have deep knowledge of the operational aspects of cybersecurity, including the types of threats and vulnerabilities that organizations face, the tools and techniques used to detect and mitigate these threats, and the practical challenges and constraints of implementing cybersecurity solutions in real-world environments. They can provide insights on how GenAI systems can be integrated into existing cybersecurity workflows and infrastructures and help ensure that these systems are effective and reliable.

Meanwhile, policymakers are experts in the legal, ethical, and societal aspects of GenAI in cybersecurity. They are responsible for setting and enforcing laws, regulations, and policies that govern the development and deployment of GenAI systems and ensuring that they are consistent with broader societal values and interests, such as privacy, security, fairness, and accountability. They can provide insights on balancing the benefits and risks of GenAI in cybersecurity. They can help ensure these systems are developed and deployed transparent, accountable, and responsive to public concerns and expectations.

Several key approaches and initiatives, including interdisciplinary research initiatives, public-private partnerships, and international cooperation and knowledge sharing, can be pursued to facilitate collaboration between these groups.

5.4.1 Interdisciplinary Research Initiatives

Interdisciplinary research initiatives are collaborative efforts that bring together researchers and experts from different fields and disciplines to work on common problems and challenges. In the context of GenAI in

5. ADDRESSING THE CHALLENGES OF GENAI IN CYBERSECURITY

cybersecurity, interdisciplinary research initiatives can help bridge the gaps between these systems' technical, operational, and policy aspects. They can facilitate the exchange of knowledge, ideas, and best practices between different communities and sectors.

Some examples of interdisciplinary research initiatives focused on GenAI in cybersecurity include:

- **The DARPA Assured Autonomy** program brings together researchers from computer science, engineering, mathematics, and other fields to develop new methods for building safe, secure, and reliable autonomous systems, including GenAI systems for cybersecurity.
- **The NSF Secure and Trustworthy Cyberspace** program funds interdisciplinary research projects exploring cybersecurity's technical, social, and policy dimensions, including projects on developing and deploying GenAI systems for threat detection, response, and mitigation.
- **The MIT-IBM Watson AI Lab** brings together researchers from MIT and IBM to work on fundamental challenges in AI, including projects focused on developing explainable, robust, and secure GenAI systems for cybersecurity and other domains.
- **The IEEE Ethics in Action** initiative brings together researchers, practitioners, and policymakers to explore AI and other emerging technologies' ethical and societal implications. Projects include those focused on responsible development and deployment of GenAI systems in cybersecurity.

To support and promote interdisciplinary research initiatives focused on GenAI in cybersecurity, organizations and stakeholders can:

- Provide funding and resources for collaborative research projects that bring together experts from different fields and sectors to work on common challenges and opportunities related to GenAI in cybersecurity.
- Establish research networks and consortia that facilitate the exchange of knowledge, data, and tools between different research groups and institutions working on GenAI in cybersecurity.
- Develop and promote standards and best practices for interdisciplinary research on GenAI in cybersecurity, including guidelines for data sharing, model documentation, and ethical review and oversight.
- Engage with policymakers and other stakeholders to ensure that interdisciplinary research initiatives are aligned with broader societal values and interests and are responsive to public concerns and expectations related to GenAI in cybersecurity.

By supporting and promoting interdisciplinary research initiatives focused on GenAI in cybersecurity, organizations and stakeholders can help accelerate the development of innovative, effective, and responsible solutions to the field's complex challenges and ensure that a diverse range informs these solutions of perspectives and expertise.

5. ADDRESSING THE CHALLENGES OF GENAI IN CYBERSECURITY

5.4.2 Public-private partnerships for responsible GenAI development

Public-private partnerships are collaborative arrangements between government agencies, private companies, and other organizations that work together to achieve common goals and objectives. In the context of GenAI in cybersecurity, public-private partnerships can help ensure that the development and deployment of these systems are informed by a broad range of stakeholder perspectives and interests and aligned with broader societal values and priorities.

Some examples of public-private partnerships focused on responsible GenAI development in cybersecurity include:

- **The National Cyber-Forensics and Training Alliance (NCFTA)** brings together law enforcement agencies, private companies, and academic institutions to share information and collaborate on cybercrime investigations and threat intelligence, including GenAI systems for threat detection and analysis.
- **The Cyber Threat Alliance (CTA)** is a nonprofit organization that brings together cybersecurity companies to share threat intelligence and collaborate on developing new tools and techniques for cyber defense, including using GenAI systems for threat hunting and incident response.
- **The Partnership on AI** is a multistakeholder organization that brings together companies, academics, and civil society groups to develop best practices and guidelines for the responsible development and deployment of AI systems, including GenAI systems in cybersecurity and other domains.
- **The NIST AI Risk Management Framework** is a voluntary frame-

work developed by the National Institute of Standards and Technology (NIST) in collaboration with private companies, academic institutions, and other stakeholders to guide the management of risks associated with the development and use of AI systems, including GenAI systems in cybersecurity.

To support and promote public-private partnerships for responsible GenAI development in cybersecurity, organizations and stakeholders can:

- Identify and engage with relevant government agencies, private companies, and other organizations involved in developing and deploying GenAI systems in cybersecurity and explore opportunities for collaboration and partnership.
- Develop and implement governance frameworks and processes for public-private partnerships that ensure transparency, accountability, and alignment with broader societal values and interests related to GenAI in cybersecurity.
- Establish clear roles, responsibilities, and expectations for each partner in the collaboration and develop mechanisms for securely and trustingly sharing data, resources, and expertise.
- Engage with the broader public and other stakeholders to ensure that public-private partnerships are responsive to public concerns and expectations related to GenAI in cybersecurity and are aligned with broader societal values and priorities.
- Monitor and evaluate the effectiveness and impact of public-private partnerships on an ongoing basis and make adjustments as needed to ensure that they continue to deliver value and benefits to all partners and stakeholders.

5. ADDRESSING THE CHALLENGES OF GENAI IN CYBERSECURITY

By supporting and promoting public-private partnerships for responsible GenAI development in cybersecurity, organizations, and stakeholders can help ensure that these systems are developed and deployed effectively, trustworthy, and aligned with broader societal values and interests. This can help build public trust and confidence in GenAI systems and ensure they are used in ways that benefit society.

5.4.3 International cooperation and knowledge sharing

International cooperation and knowledge sharing are essential for addressing the global challenges and opportunities associated with GenAI in cybersecurity. Cybersecurity threats and vulnerabilities do not respect national borders, and the development and deployment of GenAI systems in this domain require collaboration and coordination across different countries, regions, and cultures.

International cooperation and knowledge sharing can help to ensure that the benefits and risks of GenAI in cybersecurity are shared and managed fairly and equitably and that a diverse range informs the development and deployment of these systems of perspectives and experiences. They can also help to promote the development of common standards, best practices, and guidelines for the responsible development and use of GenAI in cybersecurity. They can facilitate data exchange, tools, and expertise between countries and organizations.

Some examples of international cooperation and knowledge-sharing initiatives focused on GenAI in cybersecurity include:

- **The Global Partnership on Artificial Intelligence (GPAI)** is an international initiative launched by the G7 countries to promote the responsible development and use of AI, including GenAI systems in cybersecurity and other domains. GPAI brings together government, industry, academia, and civil society experts to share knowledge and best practices and develop common approaches and standards for AI governance and ethics.

- **The United Nations Group of Governmental Experts (GGE) on Advancing Responsible State Behaviour in Cyberspace in the Context of International Security,** which is a UN-sponsored initiative that brings together experts from different countries to develop norms and principles for responsible state behavior in cyberspace, including the use of AI and other emerging technologies for cybersecurity purposes.
- **The International Telecommunication Union (ITU) AI for Good Global Summit** is an annual event that brings together AI experts, policymakers, and other stakeholders worldwide to explore AI's potential to address global challenges, including cybersecurity and digital trust.
- **The INTERPOL Global Complex for Innovation (IGCI)** is a research and development facility established by INTERPOL to support international cooperation and knowledge sharing on emerging crime threats, including threats related to AI and other advanced technologies in cybercrime and cybersecurity.

To support and promote international cooperation and knowledge sharing on GenAI in cybersecurity, organizations and stakeholders can:

- Participate in relevant international forums, conferences, and initiatives focused on GenAI in cybersecurity and contributed expertise, resources, and best practices to these efforts.

5. ADDRESSING THE CHALLENGES OF GENAI IN CYBERSECURITY

- Develop and implement international standards and guidelines for the responsible development and use of GenAI in cybersecurity in collaboration with other countries, organizations, and stakeholders.
- Establish bilateral and multilateral partnerships and agreements with other countries and organizations to share data, tools, and expertise related to GenAI in cybersecurity and to collaborate on joint research and development projects.
- Engage with international bodies and organizations, such as the United Nations, the International Telecommunication Union, and INTERPOL, to ensure that international cooperation and knowledge-sharing efforts are aligned with broader global priorities and values related to cybersecurity and digital trust.
- Monitor and evaluate the effectiveness and impact of international cooperation and knowledge-sharing initiatives on an ongoing basis, making adjustments to ensure that they continue to deliver value and benefits to all participants and stakeholders.

By supporting and promoting international cooperation and knowledge sharing on GenAI in cybersecurity, organizations, and stakeholders can help ensure that these systems are developed and deployed effectively, responsibly, and aligned with global norms and values. This can help build trust and confidence in GenAI systems across different countries and cultures and ensure they are used to benefit the international community.

6. Case Studies and Real-World Applications

To better understand the potential and challenges of GenAI in cybersecurity, it is important to examine real-world case studies and applications. In this section, we will explore successful implementations of GenAI in cybersecurity, focusing on three specific case studies: an adaptive threat intelligence platform, an automated incident response system, and a proactive vulnerability management system powered by GenAI.

6.1 Successful Implementations of GenAI in Cybersecurity

6.1.1 Case study 1: Adaptive threat intelligence platform

Threat intelligence is critical to modern cybersecurity, enabling organizations to stay informed about cybercriminals' latest threats, vulnerabilities, and attack tactics. However, traditional threat intelligence approaches often struggle to keep pace with the rapidly evolving threat landscape, relying on manual analysis and static rule-based systems to identify and prioritize threats.

6. CASE STUDIES AND REAL-WORLD APPLICATIONS

To address these challenges, some organizations have turned to GenAI-powered threat intelligence platforms that can automatically adapt to new and emerging threats in real time. One notable example of such a platform is the Adaptive Threat Intelligence (ATI) system developed by IBM Research.

The ATI system uses a combination of natural language processing (NLP), machine learning, and deep learning techniques to continuously scan and analyze vast amounts of unstructured data from various sources, including security blogs, social media, dark web forums, and threat intelligence feeds. By learning the language and context of these sources, the ATI system can identify and extract relevant threat indicators, such as malicious IP addresses, domain names, file hashes, and higher-level threat patterns and trends.

What sets the ATI system apart from traditional threat intelligence platforms is its ability to adapt and evolve its real-time threat detection and prioritization models based on feedback from human analysts and automated response systems. Using a novel approach called "reinforcement learning," the ATI system continuously optimizes its models based on the outcomes of its threat intelligence predictions, learning from successes and failures to improve its accuracy and relevance over time.

For example, suppose the ATI system generates a high-priority alert about a new ransomware campaign, but human analysts determine that the alert is a false positive. In that case, the system will automatically adjust its models to reduce the likelihood of similar false positives in the future. Conversely, suppose the ATI system correctly identifies a previously unknown threat, leading to a successful incident response. In that case, it will reinforce the models and indicators that led to that successful outcome.

The ATI system also incorporates explainable AI techniques to provide human analysts with clear and actionable insights into the reasoning behind its threat intelligence predictions. For each threat indicator or pattern identified by the system, the ATI platform generates a "threat report card" highlighting the key features and context contributing to the prediction and the threat's confidence level and potential impact.

These report cards enable human analysts to understand and validate the system's predictions quickly and provide feedback and guidance to improve the accuracy and relevance of the threat intelligence over time. By providing a clear audit trail of the data and reasoning behind each threat intelligence decision, the report cards also help build trust and accountability in the GenAI system.

Since its deployment, the ATI system has demonstrated significant benefits for organizations regarding the speed and accuracy of their threat intelligence processes. In one case study, a large financial services firm identified and responded to a previously unknown malware campaign within hours of its initial detection by the ATI platform, potentially saving millions of dollars in losses and reputational damage.

The ATI platform's success has also led to its adoption by other organizations and sectors, including government agencies, critical infrastructure providers, and managed security service providers. The platform has been recognized as a leading example of GenAI innovation in cybersecurity, winning multiple industry awards and accolades.

However, the development and deployment of the ATI platform also highlight some of the key challenges and considerations for GenAI in

6. CASE STUDIES AND REAL-WORLD APPLICATIONS

cybersecurity, particularly regarding data quality, model explainability, and human-machine collaboration.

One of the main challenges in developing the ATI system was ensuring the quality and diversity of the threat intelligence data used to train and optimize the GenAI models. To address this challenge, the IBM Research team had to develop sophisticated data pipelines and filtering mechanisms to process and curate the vast amounts of unstructured data from multiple sources while ensuring that the data was representative of the full spectrum of threats and attack vectors.

Another challenge was ensuring the explainability and interpretability of the GenAI models used in the ATI platform, particularly given the complexity and opacity of some of the deep learning techniques used. To address this challenge, the IBM Research team had to develop novel explainable AI techniques, such as the threat report cards, to provide clear and meaningful insights into the reasoning behind the system's predictions while also enabling human analysts to provide feedback and guidance to improve the models over time.

Finally, the success of the ATI platform also required close collaboration and communication between the GenAI developers, cybersecurity experts, and system end-users. The IBM Research team had to work closely with security analysts and incident responders to understand their needs and workflows and ensure the ATI platform was designed and deployed to complement and enhance their existing processes and tools.

Overall, the ATI platform demonstrates the significant potential of GenAI for transforming threat intelligence and enabling more proactive and adaptive cybersecurity. By leveraging the power of machine learning, deep learning, and reinforcement learning, the ATI system can automatically identify and prioritize emerging threats in real time while continuously adapting and improving its models based on feedback and outcomes.

At the same time, the development and deployment of the ATI platform also highlight the importance of addressing key challenges and considerations around data quality, model explainability, and human-machine collaboration in the context of GenAI for cybersecurity. As more organizations look to adopt and scale GenAI-powered threat intelligence platforms, it will be critical to learn from the successes and challenges of pioneering systems like ATI and to develop best practices and standards for responsible and effective GenAI deployment in this domain.

6.1.2 Case study 2: Automated incident response system

Incident response is critical in cybersecurity, involving detecting, investigating, and mitigating security breaches and attacks. However, traditional incident response processes rely heavily on manual analysis and decision-making by human experts, which can be time-consuming, error-prone, and difficult to scale in the face of increasing attack volumes and complexity.

To address these challenges, some organizations have turned to GenAI-powered incident response systems that automatically triage, investigate and contain security incidents in real-time. One notable example of such a system is the Autonomous Incident Response (AIR) platform developed by Darktrace, a leading provider of AI-powered cybersecurity

6. CASE STUDIES AND REAL-WORLD APPLICATIONS

solutions.

The AIR platform uses a combination of unsupervised machine learning, graph analysis, and expert system reasoning to continuously monitor an organization's digital environment for signs of malicious activity or anomalous behavior. By learning the normal activity patterns for each user, device, and application in the environment, the AIR system can quickly detect and flag any deviations or irregularities that may indicate a potential security incident.

When a potential incident is detected, the AIR platform automatically triggers a multi-stage investigation and response process, using various AI techniques to gather and analyze relevant data from across the organization's network, endpoints, and cloud services. This may include system logs, network traffic, user activity, and threat intelligence feeds, which are processed and correlated by the AIR system to build a comprehensive picture of the incident.

Based on this analysis, the AIR platform generates a detailed incident report summarizing the key findings and recommendations for response and remediation. The report includes information such as the scope and severity of the incident, the likely attack vectors and targets, the potential impact on the organization's assets and operations, and the recommended actions for containment and recovery.

The incident report is automatically routed to the appropriate security team members and stakeholders based on predefined roles and escalation protocols. The AIR platform also provides a user-friendly interface for security analysts to review and interact with the incident data, enabling them to drill down into specific details, test hypotheses, and collaborate with other team members.

In addition to its investigation and reporting capabilities, the AIR platform also includes a range of automated response actions that can be triggered based on the severity and confidence of the incident. These may include isolating infected devices, blocking malicious traffic, resetting compromised user accounts, or deploying security patches and updates.

The AIR system's built-in expert system reasoning determines the specific response actions, which applies a set of predefined rules and decision trees to evaluate the appropriate course of action based on the incident data and context. The expert system is initially trained on best practices and incident response playbooks developed by Darktrace's security experts. Still, each organization can customize and fine-tune it to reflect its specific policies, risk tolerance, and operational requirements.

One of the key benefits of the AIR platform is its ability to significantly reduce the time and effort required for incident response by automating many of the manual tasks and decision points that would otherwise require human intervention. In one case study, a global manufacturing company was able to use the AIR platform to automatically detect and contain a ransomware attack within minutes of initial compromise, preventing the spread of the malware and minimizing the impact on production systems.

The AIR platform has also demonstrated the ability to identify and respond to novel and emerging attack tactics that may evade traditional signature-based detection systems. By continuously learning and adapting to new behavior patterns, the AIR system can detect subtle and stealthy indicators of compromise that human analysts may miss, such as using living-off-the-land techniques or abusing legitimate system

6. CASE STUDIES AND REAL-WORLD APPLICATIONS

tools and services.

However, the development and deployment of the AIR platform also highlight some of the key challenges and considerations for GenAI in automated incident response. One challenge is ensuring the explainability and auditability of the AI-driven decision-making process, particularly when automated response actions that may have significant operational or business impacts are triggered.

To address this challenge, the AIR platform includes a range of explainable AI techniques, such as decision trees and rule-based reasoning, that provide transparency into the logic and evidence behind each incident response recommendation. The platform also maintains detailed audit trails and logs of all actions taken by the AI system, enabling security teams to review and validate the decisions made during an incident.

Another challenge is ensuring the robustness and resilience of the AIR platform itself, particularly in the face of adversarial attacks or evasion techniques that may seek to exploit or manipulate the AI models. To mitigate these risks, the AIR system includes a range of security controls and safeguards, such as model integrity checking, input validation, and anomaly detection, to identify and prevent any attempts to tamper with or bypass the AI decision-making process.

Finally, the success of the AIR platform also depends on effective collaboration and communication between the AI system and human security teams. While the AIR platform can automate many incident response tasks, it is not intended to entirely replace human expertise and judgment. Rather, it is designed to augment and support human analysts by providing timely, accurate, and actionable information to guide their decision-making.

To facilitate this collaboration, the AIR platform includes a range of user interface and workflow integration features that enable security teams to easily access, interpret, and act on AI-generated insights and recommendations. This may include customizable dashboards, alerts, and reports highlighting the most relevant and critical information for each user role and use case.

Overall, the AIR platform demonstrates the significant potential of GenAI for transforming incident response and enabling more automated and adaptive security operations. By leveraging the power of unsupervised learning, graph analysis, and expert system reasoning, the AIR system can automatically detect, investigate, and contain security incidents in real time while also providing explainable and auditable decision support for human analysts.

At the same time, the development and deployment of the AIR platform also highlight the importance of addressing key challenges and considerations around explainability, robustness, and human-machine collaboration in the context of GenAI for incident response. As more organizations look to adopt and scale GenAI-powered incident response systems, it will be critical to learn from the successes and challenges of pioneering platforms like AIR and to develop best practices and standards for responsible and effective GenAI deployment in this domain.

6.1.3 Case study 3: Proactive vulnerability management with GenAI

Vulnerability management is another critical function in cybersecurity. It involves identifying, prioritizing, and remedying security weaknesses and exposures in an organization's systems and applications. However, traditional vulnerability management approaches often struggle to keep pace with the rapidly evolving threat landscape, relying on periodic scans and manual prioritization to identify and fix vulnerabilities.

To address these challenges, some organizations have turned to GenAI-powered vulnerability management systems that can proactively identify and prioritize vulnerabilities based on their likelihood and potential impact of exploitation. One notable example of such a system is the Predictive Vulnerability Management (PVM) platform developed by Balbix, a leading AI-powered cybersecurity risk management solutions provider.

The PVM platform uses machine learning, natural language processing, and simulation techniques to continuously assess and predict the risk of vulnerabilities across an organization's entire attack surface, including on-premises, cloud, and mobile assets. By ingesting and analyzing data from various sources, such as vulnerability scanners, asset inventories, threat intelligence feeds, and security policies, the PVM system can build a comprehensive and dynamic view of an organization's vulnerability landscape.

One of the key innovations of the PVM platform is its use of generative adversarial networks (GANs) to simulate and predict the behavior of potential attackers. GANs are a type of deep learning architecture that consists of two neural networks - a generator and a discriminator - that compete against each other to create realistic and diverse examples of a given data distribution.

In vulnerability management, the PVM platform uses GANs to generate realistic attack scenarios and exploit chains that mimic the tactics and techniques used by real-world adversaries. By training the generator network on a large corpus of historical attack data and threat intelligence, the PVM system can learn to create novel and diverse attack scenarios that may not have been seen before but are plausible, given the current state of an organization's vulnerabilities and defenses.

On the other hand, the discriminator network is trained to distinguish between real and generated attack scenarios, providing feedback to the generator on improving the realism and effectiveness of its simulations. The PVM platform can continuously refine and adapt its vulnerability risk models based on the latest threat intelligence and attack trends through this iterative process.

Based on these simulated attack scenarios, the PVM platform generates a prioritized list of vulnerabilities and recommended remediation actions, considering factors such as the likelihood and impact of exploitation, the criticality of affected assets, and the feasibility and cost of remediation. The platform also provides a user-friendly interface for security teams to visualize and explore the vulnerability risk data, enabling them to drill down into specific assets, vulnerabilities, and attack paths.

One of the key benefits of the PVM platform is its ability to provide a more proactive and risk-based approach to vulnerability management by identifying and prioritizing vulnerabilities based on their actual

6. CASE STUDIES AND REAL-WORLD APPLICATIONS

likelihood and potential impact of exploitation rather than just their technical severity or age. In one case study, a large financial services firm was able to use the PVM platform to reduce its vulnerability risk exposure by over 60% within the first six months of deployment by focusing remediation efforts on the most critical and likely-to-be-exploited vulnerabilities.

The PVM platform has also demonstrated the ability to identify and prioritize zero-day vulnerabilities and emerging attack vectors that traditional vulnerability scanners or threat intelligence feeds may not detect. By continuously simulating and predicting the behavior of potential attackers, the PVM system can identify weaknesses and exposures in an organization's defenses that may not be apparent from a purely technical or signature-based perspective.

However, the development and deployment of the PVM platform also highlight some of the key challenges and considerations for GenAI in proactive vulnerability management. One challenge is ensuring the accuracy and reliability of the AI-generated vulnerability risk predictions, particularly given the complexity and uncertainty of real-world attack scenarios.

To address this challenge, the PVM platform includes a range of validation and testing techniques, such as cross-validation, sensitivity analysis, and human expert review, to assess and improve the performance of its vulnerability risk models. The platform also provides transparency into its simulations' underlying data and assumptions, enabling security teams to understand and trust the AI-generated risk predictions.

Another challenge is ensuring the scalability and efficiency of the PVM platform, particularly in large and complex enterprise environments with thousands of assets and vulnerabilities. To address this challenge, the PVM platform includes a range of optimization and parallelization techniques, such as distributed computing, incremental learning, and active learning, to enable the system to process and analyze large volumes of vulnerability data in real time.

Finally, the success of the PVM platform also depends on effective integration and collaboration with existing vulnerability management processes and tools. While the PVM platform can provide valuable insights and recommendations for vulnerability prioritization and remediation, it is not intended to replace existing scanners, patching systems, or ticketing workflows entirely. Rather, it is designed to complement and enhance these tools by providing a more risk-based and predictive approach to vulnerability management.

To facilitate this integration, the PVM platform includes a range of API and plugin integrations with popular vulnerability management and IT service management tools, such as Qualys, Rapid7, ServiceNow, and Jira. This enables security teams to easily import and export vulnerability data between the PVM platform and their existing tools and incorporate AI-generated risk insights and recommendations into their day-to-day vulnerability management workflows.

Overall, the PVM platform demonstrates the significant potential of GenAI for transforming vulnerability management and enabling more proactive and risk-based security operations. By leveraging the power of generative adversarial networks, machine learning, and simulation techniques, the PVM system can automatically identify and prioritize vulnerabilities based on their likelihood and potential impact of exploitation while also adapting to new and emerging attack vectors.

6. CASE STUDIES AND REAL-WORLD APPLICATIONS

At the same time, the development and deployment of the PVM platform also highlight the importance of addressing key challenges and considerations around accuracy, scalability, and integration in the context of GenAI for vulnerability management. As more organizations look to adopt and scale GenAI-powered vulnerability management systems, it will be critical to learn from the successes and challenges of pioneering platforms like PVM and to develop best practices and standards for responsible and effective GenAI deployment in this domain.

6.2 Lessons Learned from GenAI Failures or Misuse in Cybersecurity

While the previous case studies highlighted successful implementations of GenAI in cybersecurity, examining instances where GenAI has failed or been misused in this domain is equally important. By learning from these negative examples, we can identify potential pitfalls and challenges in developing and deploying GenAI systems and develop strategies to mitigate these risks in future applications.

This section will explore three examples of GenAI failures or misuse in cybersecurity: biased threat detection leading to false positives, lack of explainability in automated decision-making, and ethical concerns in GenAI-powered surveillance.

6.2.1 Example 1: Biased threat detection leading to false positives

One of the most common failures of GenAI in cybersecurity is the presence of bias in threat detection models, leading to high rates of false positives and negatives. False positives occur when a GenAI system incorrectly identifies a benign activity or entity as malicious, while false negatives occur when a real threat is missed or overlooked.

Biased threat detection can arise from various sources, such as biased training data, flawed model architectures, or inappropriate evaluation metrics. For example, suppose a GenAI system is trained on a dataset skewed towards certain types of threats or attack vectors. In that case, it may develop a bias toward detecting those specific patterns while missing other threats that are underrepresented in the training data.

One notable example of biased threat detection occurred in the context of a GenAI-powered email security system deployed by a large financial institution. The system used a deep learning model to classify incoming emails as legitimate or malicious based on various features such as sender reputation, content analysis, and attachment characteristics.

However, after several months of operation, the security team noticed the system generated many false positives for emails from certain geographic regions and domains. Upon further investigation, they discovered that the training data used to develop the model significantly overrepresented malicious emails from those specific regions and domains, leading the model to develop a bias toward classifying any email from those sources as a potential threat.

As a result, the system incorrectly flagged many legitimate business emails as malicious, causing significant disruption to the organization's communication and productivity. In some cases, important client emails were blocked or quarantined, leading to missed opportunities and damaged relationships.

To address this issue, the security team had to retrain the model on a more diverse and representative dataset, using data augmentation, oversampling, and undersampling to balance the distribution of different threat types and sources. They also implemented additional safeguards and monitoring processes to detect and mitigate potential biases in the model's predictions over time.

This example highlights the importance of ensuring the quality, diversity, and representativeness of training data in the development of GenAI systems for cybersecurity. It also underscores the need for continuous testing, validation, and monitoring of these systems to identify and address any biases or anomalies that may emerge in real-world deployments.

6.2.2 Example 2: Lack of explainability in automated decision-making

Another common failure of GenAI in cybersecurity is the lack of explainability and transparency in automated decision-making processes. Many GenAI systems, particularly those based on deep learning architectures, can be highly complex and opaque, making it difficult for human operators to understand how and why certain decisions or actions are being taken.

This lack of explainability can be particularly problematic in high-stakes cybersecurity applications, where the consequences of incorrect or inappropriate decisions can be severe. For example, suppose a GenAI system automatically blocks or terminates a critical business process or system based on a false positive threat detection. In that case, it can cause an organization significant operational and financial damage.

One notable example of this occurred in the context of a GenAI-powered network security system deployed by a large healthcare provider. The system used a combination of machine learning and rule-based algorithms to continuously monitor network traffic and automatically block any suspicious or anomalous activity.

However, during a routine maintenance window, the GenAI system suddenly began blocking all traffic to and from a critical patient monitoring system, causing it to go offline and triggering alarms and panic among the clinical staff. The security team was initially unable to determine the cause of the blocking, as the GenAI system did not provide any clear explanation or rationale for its decision.

After several hours of investigation and troubleshooting, the team finally discovered that the GenAI system had detected a sudden spike in traffic to the patient monitoring system during the maintenance window, which it had interpreted as a potential denial-of-service attack. However, the traffic spike was caused by a scheduled data synchronization process initiated by the maintenance team.

The security team could not diagnose and resolve the issue quickly because the GenAI system could not explain its decision-making process or provide any contextual information about the detected anomaly. As a result, the patient monitoring system remained offline for an extended period, potentially putting patient safety and well-being at risk.

The healthcare provider worked with the GenAI system vendor to address this issue by implementing additional explainability and transparency features, such as decision trees, rule tracing, and contextual alerts. These features gave human operators more visibility and control over the system's automated decision-making processes, enabling them to identify and override any incorrect or inappropriate actions quickly.

This example highlights the importance of ensuring that GenAI systems in cybersecurity are designed with explainability and transparency in mind, particularly when used to automate high-stakes decisions or actions. It also underscores the need for human oversight and intervention in these systems to ensure that the AI operates safely, reliably, and accountable.

6.2.3 Example 3: Ethical concerns in GenAI-powered surveillance

A third example of GenAI failure or misuse in cybersecurity concerns ethical concerns around using these technologies for surveillance and monitoring purposes. While GenAI can be a powerful tool for detecting and preventing cyber threats, it can also be used in ways that violate individual privacy, civil liberties, and human rights.

One notable example of this occurred in the context of a GenAI-powered facial recognition system deployed by a law enforcement agency to monitor public spaces for potential criminal activity. The system used deep learning algorithms to analyze video feeds from surveillance cameras and automatically identify and track individuals based on their facial features and movements.

However, it was later revealed that the GenAI system had been trained on a biased and unrepresentative dataset, which significantly overrepresented individuals from certain racial and ethnic groups. As a result, the system disproportionately targeted and flagged these individuals as potential suspects, even when they had not engaged in any criminal activity.

In addition, the law enforcement agency deployed the GenAI system without adequate transparency, oversight, or accountability measures. There were no clear policies or guidelines governing its use, and individuals targeted by the system had no way of knowing or challenging the basis for their surveillance.

When civil liberties groups and media investigations brought these issues to light, it sparked significant public outcry and criticism of the law enforcement agency and the GenAI vendor. The agency was forced to suspend the use of the facial recognition system pending a full review and investigation of its practices, and the vendor faced legal and reputational consequences for its role in developing and deploying the biased system.

This example highlights the importance of considering the ethical and societal implications of GenAI systems in cybersecurity, particularly when used for surveillance or monitoring purposes. It underscores the need for clear policies, guidelines, and oversight mechanisms to ensure these systems are used fairly, transparently, and accountable.

6. CASE STUDIES AND REAL-WORLD APPLICATIONS

They do not violate individual rights or perpetuate systemic biases and inequalities.

Organizations developing and deploying GenAI systems in cybersecurity should adopt a proactive and multi-stakeholder approach to ethics and governance to address these concerns. This may involve engaging with diverse communities and advocacy groups to understand their perspectives and concerns, conducting regular audits and assessments of GenAI systems to identify and mitigate any biases or unintended consequences, and establishing clear processes for individuals to challenge or appeal decisions made by these systems.

Overall, these examples of GenAI failures and misuse in cybersecurity underscore the importance of approaching the development and deployment of these technologies with caution, humility, and a commitment to ongoing learning and improvement. While GenAI can potentially transform cybersecurity positively and more powerfully, it is not a panacea or a replacement for human judgment and oversight.

By learning from these negative examples and incorporating the lessons into future GenAI applications, we can work towards building more robust, reliable, and ethical AI systems that enhance rather than undermine cybersecurity and human values.

6.3 Future Directions and Emerging Trends

As the field of GenAI in cybersecurity continues to evolve and mature, it is important to consider the future directions and emerging trends that will shape the development and deployment of these technologies in the coming years. In this section, we will explore three key areas of future growth and innovation: the integration of GenAI with other emerging technologies such as blockchain and 5G, the challenges and opportunities of adversarial AI and the evolving threat landscape, and the potential for personalized and context-aware cybersecurity with GenAI.

6.3.1 Integration of GenAI with other emerging technologies (e.g., blockchain, 5G)

One of the most promising future directions for GenAI in cybersecurity is the integration of these technologies with other emerging technologies, such as blockchain and 5G networks. By combining the power of GenAI with the unique capabilities and characteristics of these technologies, we can create new and innovative approaches to cybersecurity that are more secure, resilient, and adaptive to the changing threat landscape.

For example, integrating GenAI with blockchain technology could enable developing more secure and decentralized systems for threat intelligence sharing and collaboration. Blockchain's distributed ledger technology provides a tamper-proof and immutable record of transactions and data, which could be used to securely store and share threat indicators, attack signatures, and other cybersecurity data across multiple organizations and jurisdictions.

GenAI could analyze this blockchain-based threat intelligence data in real-time, identifying patterns and correlations that might indicate the presence of coordinated or large-scale attacks. By leveraging multiple organizations' collective intelligence and resources, GenAI-

6. CASE STUDIES AND REAL-WORLD APPLICATIONS

blockchain systems could provide a more comprehensive and proactive defense against cyber threats, reducing the risk of successful attacks and minimizing the impact of incidents when they occur.

Another example of integrating GenAI with emerging technologies is using these systems in the context of 5G networks and the Internet of Things (IoT). 5G networks promise to deliver faster, more reliable, and more ubiquitous connectivity than previous generations of mobile networks, enabling a wide range of new applications and services in areas such as smart cities, autonomous vehicles, and industrial automation.

However, the increased connectivity and complexity of 5G networks also create new cybersecurity risks and challenges, such as the potential for large-scale DDoS attacks, exploiting vulnerabilities in IoT devices, and compromising critical infrastructure systems. GenAI could play a key role in addressing these challenges by providing real-time monitoring, anomaly detection, and threat response capabilities tailored to the unique characteristics and requirements of 5G networks.

For example, GenAI systems could be used to analyze the massive volumes of data generated by 5G-connected devices and applications, identifying patterns and anomalies that might indicate the presence of malicious activity or vulnerabilities. These systems could also be used to automatically generate and deploy security policies and configurations optimized for the specific needs and constraints of 5G networks, such as low-latency and high-bandwidth applications.

By integrating GenAI with the capabilities of 5G networks and IoT devices, we can create more intelligent, adaptive, and autonomous cybersecurity systems to protect against a wide range of threats and attacks. However, developing and deploying these integrated systems will require close collaboration and coordination between experts in AI, cybersecurity, telecommunications, and other relevant domains and the development of new standards, frameworks, and best practices for secure and responsible AI integration.

6.3.2 Adversarial AI and the evolving threat landscape

Another key future direction for GenAI in cybersecurity is the challenges and opportunities posed by adversarial AI and the evolving threat landscape. As GenAI systems become more sophisticated and widely deployed in cybersecurity applications, they also become a more attractive target for adversaries seeking to exploit or manipulate these systems for malicious purposes.

Adversarial AI uses AI techniques and methods to attack, deceive, or manipulate AI systems, often by exploiting vulnerabilities or biases in the underlying algorithms or data. For example, an adversary could use specially crafted input data or perturbations to cause a GenAI-based malware detection system to misclassify malicious files as benign or to evade detection altogether.

As the capabilities and prevalence of GenAI in cybersecurity continue to grow, so will the sophistication and frequency of adversarial AI attacks. Adversaries may seek to use GenAI techniques to automate and scale their attacks, create more realistic and persuasive phishing emails or social engineering scams, or develop new and novel attack vectors specifically designed to exploit the weaknesses of AI systems.

6. CASE STUDIES AND REAL-WORLD APPLICATIONS

The cybersecurity community must develop new and innovative approaches to adversarial AI defense and resilience to address these challenges. This may involve creating more robust and adaptive AI algorithms that can detect and respond to adversarial inputs and manipulations and using adversarial training, input validation, and runtime monitoring to harden AI systems against attacks.

It may also involve the development of new collaboration and information-sharing mechanisms that allow cybersecurity organizations to share knowledge and intelligence about emerging adversarial AI threats and techniques and coordinate their efforts to detect and mitigate these threats. This could include the creation of shared databases and repositories of adversarial AI examples and signatures, as well as the development of standardized frameworks and protocols for sharing and analyzing this information.

Another key aspect of addressing the challenges of adversarial AI and the evolving threat landscape will be the development of more explainable, transparent, and accountable AI systems. As discussed in previous sections, the lack of transparency and explainability in many GenAI systems can make it difficult for human operators to understand and trust the decisions and actions of these systems, particularly in the context of high-stakes cybersecurity applications.

By developing GenAI systems that are more transparent and interpretable and that provide clear explanations and audit trails for their decisions and actions, we can help build trust and confidence in these systems and enable more effective human oversight and intervention when necessary. This may involve techniques such as feature importance analysis, rule extraction, counterfactual explanations, and developing standardized frameworks and guidelines for AI explainability and transparency in cybersecurity.

Overall, the challenges and opportunities of adversarial AI and the evolving threat landscape will require a proactive, collaborative, and multi-disciplinary approach from the cybersecurity community. By bringing together experts in AI, cybersecurity, ethics, and other relevant domains and by developing new technologies, frameworks, and best practices for secure and responsible AI development and deployment, we can work towards a future in which GenAI systems are a powerful and trusted tool for enhancing cybersecurity and protecting against evolving threats.

6.3.3 Personalized and context-aware cybersecurity with GenAI

A third key future direction for GenAI in cybersecurity is the potential for these technologies to enable more personalized and context-aware approaches to cybersecurity. As the complexity and diversity of cyber threats continue to grow, it is becoming increasingly important for cybersecurity systems to be able to adapt and respond to the unique needs, preferences, and contexts of individual users and organizations.

GenAI techniques such as deep learning, transfer learning, and reinforcement learning could play a key role in enabling these more personalized and adaptive approaches to cybersecurity. For example, GenAI systems could analyze user behavior and activity patterns over time, building individualized models of normal and anomalous behavior tailored to each user's specific needs and contexts.

6. CASE STUDIES AND REAL-WORLD APPLICATIONS

These personalized behavior models could then detect and respond to potential security threats in real time, providing more accurate and targeted alerts and interventions than traditional rule-based or signature-based approaches. For example, if a user suddenly starts accessing sensitive data or systems at unusual times or from distinctive locations, a GenAI-based anomaly detection system could flag this behavior as a potential security risk and prompt the user to provide additional authentication or verification.

GenAI systems could also provide users with more personalized and context-aware security recommendations and guidance based on their risk profiles, preferences, and behaviors. For example, a GenAI-based security assistant could analyze a user's browsing and email habits and provide tailored recommendations for improving their security hygiene, such as suggesting a password manager or warning them about potential phishing attempts.

In addition to providing more personalized security for individual users, GenAI techniques could also enable more context-aware and adaptive security policies and controls at the organizational level. For example, a GenAI system could continuously monitor and analyze an organization's network traffic and user activity, identifying patterns and anomalies that might indicate the presence of a security threat or vulnerability.

Based on this analysis, the GenAI system could automatically generate and implement dynamic security policies and configurations optimized for the organization's specific needs and risks at any given time. For example, if the system detects a sudden increase in network traffic from a particular geographic region or a spike in user activity outside of normal business hours, it could automatically adjust firewall rules or access controls to mitigate potential threats.

Developing and deploying these more personalized and context-aware approaches to cybersecurity with GenAI will require several key enabling technologies and frameworks. These may include:

- Advanced data collection and analytics platforms that can process and analyze large volumes of heterogeneous security data in real time, such as network logs, endpoint telemetry, and user activity data.
- Secure and privacy-preserving machine learning techniques that can enable the training and deployment of personalized GenAI models without compromising the confidentiality or integrity of sensitive user data.
- Explainable and transparent AI frameworks that can provide clear and interpretable explanations for the decisions and actions of GenAI-based security systems, enabling users and administrators to understand and trust these systems.
- Adaptive and resilient security architectures that can dynamically reconfigure and optimize security controls and policies based on users' and organizations' evolving needs and contexts.
- Collaborative and multi-stakeholder approaches to AI governance and ethics in cybersecurity ensure that principles of fairness, accountability, and transparency guide the development and deployment of these technologies.

As GenAI technologies continue to advance and mature, the potential for more personalized and context-aware approaches to cybersecurity will only continue to grow. By leveraging the power of these technologies to build more intelligent, adaptive, and human-centric security systems,

6. CASE STUDIES AND REAL-WORLD APPLICATIONS

we can work towards a future in which individuals and organizations are better protected against the ever-evolving landscape of cyber threats.

However, the development and deployment of these GenAI-enabled approaches to cybersecurity will also raise important ethical and societal questions that must be carefully considered and addressed. These may include concerns around privacy, bias, the potential for these technologies to be used for surveillance or other malicious purposes, and questions around the appropriate balance between automated decision-making and human oversight and control.

Addressing these challenges will require ongoing collaboration and dialogue between experts in AI, cybersecurity, ethics, and other relevant domains, as well as the active engagement and participation of users, organizations, and other stakeholders in developing and governance these technologies. By working together to create secure, responsible, and trustworthy approaches to personalized and context-aware cybersecurity with GenAI, we can help build a more resilient and adaptive security ecosystem that can effectively protect against the threats of today and tomorrow.

7. Conclusion

Throughout this book, we have explored the potential of Generative AI (GenAI) to revolutionize cybersecurity. GenAI technologies offer a wide range of promising applications and benefits for organizations seeking to strengthen their cyber defenses and resilience, from enhancing threat detection and prevention to automating incident response and improving vulnerability management.

However, we have also examined the risks, challenges, and ethical considerations of developing and deploying GenAI in cybersecurity. These include concerns around bias and fairness, explainability and interpretability, accountability and responsibility, and potential misuse or unintended consequences.

As we conclude our exploration of AI-powered cybersecurity, it is important to reflect on these potential benefits and risks and consider how we can work towards a future in which GenAI technologies are developed and deployed responsibly, transparently, and human-centric.

7. CONCLUSION

7.1 Balancing the Benefits and Risks of GenAI in Cybersecurity

7.1.1 Recap of the promise and perils discussed in the book

The previous chapters examined how GenAI technologies can be leveraged to enhance and transform various aspects of cybersecurity. Some of the key benefits and opportunities we have discussed include:

- Enhancing threat detection and prevention: GenAI techniques such as anomaly detection, malware analysis, and intrusion detection can help organizations to identify and respond to cyber threats more quickly and accurately than traditional rule-based or signature-based approaches. By learning patterns and anomalies from large volumes of security data, GenAI systems can adapt to new and evolving threats in real time, providing a more proactive and dynamic defense against cyber attacks.

- **Automating incident response and remediation:** GenAI technologies can automate and streamline various aspects of incident response, from generating playbooks and containment actions to adapting response strategies based on each incident's specific characteristics and context. By reducing the manual effort and time required to investigate and mitigate security incidents, GenAI can help organizations minimize the impact and cost of cyber attacks.
- **Improving vulnerability management and risk assessment:** GenAI techniques such as attack simulation and prioritization can help organizations identify and prioritize the most critical and likely-to-be-exploited vulnerabilities in their systems and networks. By generating realistic attack scenarios and predicting the potential

impact of different vulnerabilities, GenAI can enable a more proactive and risk-based approach to vulnerability management.
- **Streamlining security operations and reducing human error:** GenAI technologies can automate repetitive and time-consuming security tasks, such as alert triage, incident reporting, and compliance monitoring. By augmenting human decision-making with intelligent insights and recommendations, GenAI can help reduce the risk of human error and cognitive biases in security operations.

However, we have also explored the various risks and challenges associated with the use of GenAI in cybersecurity, including:

- **Bias and fairness concerns:** GenAI systems can inherit and amplify biases in the data used to train them, leading to discriminatory or unfair outcomes in cybersecurity applications. This can result in disproportionate false positive rates for certain groups or individuals or perpetuate systemic inequalities in access to cybersecurity resources and protection.
- **Explainability and interpretability challenges:** Many GenAI technologies, particularly those based on deep learning architectures, can be difficult to interpret and explain, making it challenging for human operators to understand and trust these systems' decisions and actions. This lack of transparency can hinder effective collaboration between human and AI decision-makers and make it difficult to audit and evaluate the performance of GenAI systems over time.
- **Accountability and ethical considerations:** GenAI in cybersecurity raises important questions around accountability, responsibility, and liability in case of system failures, errors, or unintended consequences. There are also concerns about the potential misuse of GenAI technologies for surveillance, profiling, or other unethical

purposes, particularly in the absence of clear governance frameworks and ethical guidelines.
- **Adversarial attacks and robustness challenges:** As GenAI systems become more prevalent in cybersecurity applications, they may also become a target for adversarial attacks designed to deceive, manipulate, or exploit these systems. Ensuring the robustness and resilience of GenAI technologies against such attacks is a critical challenge requiring ongoing research and innovation.

7.1.2 The need for a responsible and human-centric approach

Given the complex interplay of benefits and risks associated with GenAI in cybersecurity, it is clear that a responsible, transparent, and human-centric approach must guide the development and deployment of these technologies. This means that the potential impacts and implications of GenAI must be carefully considered and addressed at every stage of the AI lifecycle, from initial research and design to deployment and ongoing monitoring and evaluation.

Some key principles and practices that can help to promote a responsible and human-centric approach to GenAI in cybersecurity include:

- Ensuring diversity and inclusivity in the development and governance of GenAI technologies by involving a wide range of stakeholders and perspectives in the design, testing, and oversight of these systems.
- Prioritizing transparency and explainability in the development

and deployment of GenAI systems by using techniques such as feature importance analysis, rule extraction, and counterfactual explanations to provide clear and interpretable insights into the decision-making processes of these systems.
- Establishing clear accountability and responsibility frameworks for using GenAI in cybersecurity, defining roles and responsibilities for different stakeholders, and implementing mechanisms for auditing, monitoring, and redressing errors, biases, or unintended consequences.
- Incorporating human oversight and control into the operation of GenAI systems by designing these technologies to augment and support human decision-making rather than replacing it entirely and ensuring that there are always clear mechanisms for human intervention and override when necessary.
- Developing and enforcing robust ethical guidelines and principles for using GenAI in cybersecurity based on fairness, transparency, accountability, and respect for human rights and dignity.
- Fostering ongoing collaboration and knowledge-sharing between experts in AI, cybersecurity, ethics, and other relevant domains to ensure that diverse perspectives and expertise inform the development and deployment of GenAI technologies.
- Investing in research and innovation to address key technical challenges and limitations of GenAI systems, such as improving robustness against adversarial attacks, enhancing explainability and interpretability, and ensuring the scalability and efficiency of these technologies in real-world settings.

By adopting these and other responsible AI practices, organizations can work towards realizing the full potential of GenAI in cybersecurity while mitigating the risks and challenges associated with these technologies. This will require a sustained commitment to collaboration, transparency, and ethical reflection from all stakeholders involved in the development and deployment of GenAI systems, as well as a willingness to adapt and evolve these approaches in response to new insights, experiences, and challenges.

Ultimately, a responsible and human-centric approach to GenAI in cybersecurity aims not to eliminate all risks or achieve perfect security but to ensure that these technologies are developed and used consistently with human values, rights, and interests. By striving towards this goal, we can help build a future in which GenAI is a powerful and trusted tool for enhancing cybersecurity and protecting individuals, organizations, and society from the ever-evolving landscape of cyber threats.

7.2 Recommendations for Responsible Development and Deployment of GenAI

As we have seen throughout this book, the development, and deployment of GenAI technologies in cybersecurity is a complex and multifaceted challenge that requires careful consideration and ongoing collaboration from a wide range of stakeholders. This section will provide some concrete recommendations, actionable steps for organizations seeking to adopt GenAI in their cybersecurity practices, and broader policy recommendations for regulators and decision-makers looking to promote responsible and effective use of these technologies.

7.2.1 Actionable steps for organizations adopting GenAI in cybersecurity

For organizations that are considering or already implementing GenAI technologies in their cybersecurity operations, there are several key steps and best practices that can help to ensure the responsible and effective deployment of these systems:

1. **Clearly define the goals and scope of GenAI adoption:** Before embarking on any GenAI project, it is important to clearly understand the specific cybersecurity challenges and use cases these technologies intend to address. This involves defining measurable objectives and success criteria and identifying any constraints or limitations that may impact the feasibility or effectiveness of GenAI solutions.

2. **Assess and mitigate potential risks and biases:** As discussed in previous chapters, GenAI systems can be susceptible to various forms of prejudice and unfairness, leading to discriminatory or harmful outcomes in cybersecurity applications. To mitigate these risks, organizations should conduct thorough assessments of the data, algorithms, and processes used to train and deploy GenAI models and implement strategies such as data diversification, fairness-aware model design, and continuous monitoring and auditing for bias.

3. **Ensure transparency and explainability of GenAI systems:** To promote trust and accountability in using GenAI for cybersecurity, it is essential to provide clear and interpretable explanations of how these systems make decisions and take action. This can involve techniques such as feature importance analysis, rule extraction, counterfactual reasoning, and human-readable interfaces and visualizations to convey

complex GenAI insights in an accessible and understandable way.

4. Implement human oversight and control mechanisms: While GenAI technologies can automate and augment many aspects of cybersecurity operations, it is important to ensure that there are always clear mechanisms for human oversight, intervention, and control. This may involve designing GenAI systems with built-in "human-in-the-loop" checkpoints, establishing clear escalation and override protocols, and providing training and support to help human operators effectively collaborate with and manage GenAI technologies.

5. Foster a culture of responsible AI and continuous learning: Adopting GenAI in cybersecurity is not a one-time event but an ongoing learning, adaptation, and improvement process. Organizations should strive to cultivate a culture of responsible AI development and deployment, in which ethical considerations, transparency, and accountability are prioritized at every stage of the AI lifecycle. This may involve providing training and resources to help employees understand and apply responsible AI practices and establishing feedback loops and mechanisms for continuous monitoring, evaluation, and refinement of GenAI systems over time.

6. Collaborate with diverse stakeholders and domain experts: The development and deployment of GenAI technologies in cybersecurity is a complex and interdisciplinary challenge requiring input and collaboration from various stakeholders and domain experts. Organizations should seek partnerships and collaborations with researchers, vendors, regulators, and other relevant parties to share knowledge, best practices, and resources for responsible GenAI adoption. This can help to ensure that GenAI solutions are informed by diverse perspectives and expertise and are aligned with broader societal values and priorities.

7. Plan for long-term sustainability and resilience: As GenAI technologies become more integrated into cybersecurity operations, it is important to consider these systems' long-term sustainability and resilience. This may involve developing strategies for managing the lifecycle of GenAI models, including regular updating, retraining, and retirement as needed, as well as establishing contingency plans and fallback mechanisms in case of system failures or disruptions. Organizations should also consider the broader societal and environmental impacts of GenAI adoption and strive to develop effective, efficient, sustainable, and equitable solutions in the long run.

By following these recommendations and best practices, organizations can work towards the responsible and effective adoption of GenAI technologies in their cybersecurity operations while contributing to the broader ecosystem of responsible AI development and deployment.

7.2.2 Policy recommendations for regulators and decision-makers

In addition to the steps that individual organizations can take to promote responsible GenAI adoption in cybersecurity, regulators, policymakers, and other decision-makers also play a critical role in shaping the broader landscape of GenAI governance and oversight. Some key policy recommendations for these stakeholders include:

1. Develop clear and consistent regulatory frameworks for GenAI in cybersecurity: To provide clarity and certainty for organizations developing and deploying GenAI technologies, regulators should work towards establishing clear and consistent regulatory frameworks that define the roles, responsibilities, and expectations for different stakeholders involved in the GenAI ecosystem. This may involve adapting existing regulations and guidelines related to cybersecurity, data protection, and AI governance, as well as developing new standards and best practices specifically tailored to the unique challenges and opportunities of GenAI in cybersecurity.

2. Promote transparency and accountability in GenAI development and deployment: Regulators and policymakers should prioritize transparency and accountability as core principles of GenAI governance and work to establish mechanisms and incentives that encourage organizations to adopt responsible AI practices. This may involve requiring organizations to disclose key information about their GenAI systems, such as the data and algorithms used in training and deployment, and establishing oversight and enforcement mechanisms to ensure compliance with relevant regulations and standards.

3. Foster multi-stakeholder collaboration and knowledge-sharing: Given the complex and interdisciplinary nature of GenAI in cybersecurity, it is essential to promote collaboration and knowledge-sharing among diverse stakeholders, including researchers, practitioners, policymakers, and civil society organizations. Regulators and decision-makers can play a key role in facilitating these collaborations by convening multi-stakeholder forums and initiatives, providing funding and resources for collaborative research and development, and encouraging sharing of data, tools, and best practices across different domains and sectors.

4. Address potential risks and unintended consequences of GenAI adoption: As GenAI technologies become more prevalent in cybersecurity and other domains, it is important to proactively identify and address potential risks and unintended consequences that may arise from their use. This may involve conducting impact assessments and risk analyses to identify potential harms and vulnerabilities and developing strategies and safeguards to mitigate these risks. Regulators and policymakers should also consider the broader societal implications of GenAI adoption, such as the potential for job displacement, privacy erosion, or the exacerbation of existing inequalities, and work to develop policies and programs that promote equitable and inclusive outcomes.

5. Invest in research and education to build GenAI capacity and expertise: To support the responsible development and deployment of GenAI technologies in cybersecurity and beyond, investing in research and education initiatives that can make the necessary capacity and expertise in this field is essential. This may involve funding basic and applied research in GenAI and related domains, supporting the development of educational programs and curricula focused on responsible AI, and providing training and resources to help organizations and individuals acquire the skills and knowledge needed to develop, deploy, and manage GenAI systems effectively.

6. Engage in international cooperation and harmonization efforts: As GenAI technologies become more globalized and interconnected, regulators and policymakers must engage in international cooperation and harmonization efforts to promote consistent and effective governance approaches across different jurisdictions and regions. This may involve participating in international forums and initiatives related to AI governance and cybersecurity, such as the OECD AI Principles or the UN Group of Governmental Experts on Advancing Responsible State Behavior in Cyberspace, as well as working to align domestic policies and regulations with emerging global standards and best practices.

By implementing these and other policy recommendations, regulators and decision-makers can help create an enabling environment for responsible development and deployment of GenAI technologies in cybersecurity while promoting broader societal values such as transparency, accountability, fairness, and inclusivity. As the GenAI landscape continues to evolve and mature, it will be essential for these stakeholders to remain proactive and adaptive in their approaches to governance and oversight and to work collaboratively with other actors in the ecosystem to address the complex challenges and opportunities that lie ahead.

7.3 The Future of AI-powered Cybersecurity and its Implications for Society

As we have explored throughout this book, integrating GenAI technologies into cybersecurity practices has the potential to fundamentally transform how we detect, prevent, and respond to cyber threats. However, the implications of this transformation extend far beyond the technical domain of cybersecurity itself and are likely to have significant and far-reaching impacts on society as a whole.

In this final section, we will consider some potential long-term impacts of AI-powered cybersecurity on the cybersecurity industry and the broader societal implications of these technologies. We will also emphasize the need for ongoing dialogue and collaboration among diverse stakeholders to ensure that a strong ethical framework and a commitment to the public good guide the development and deployment of GenAI in cybersecurity.

7.3.1 Potential long-term impacts on the cybersecurity industry

Adopting GenAI technologies in cybersecurity will likely significantly impact the cybersecurity industry's structure, practices, and workforce. Some of the potential impacts include:

1. **Automation and augmentation of cybersecurity tasks:** As GenAI technologies become more sophisticated and capable, they will likely automate and augment an increasing range of cybersecurity tasks, from threat detection and analysis to incident response and remediation. This could lead to significant improvements in the speed, accuracy, and efficiency of cybersecurity operations but may also require substantial changes in cybersecurity professionals' roles, skills, and workflows.

2. **Shift towards proactive and predictive security:** GenAI technologies' ability to learn from vast amounts of data and adapt to evolving threat landscapes could enable a shift towards more proactive and predictive approaches to cybersecurity. Rather than reacting to threats after they have already occurred, GenAI-powered systems may be able to anticipate and prevent potential attacks before they can cause damage. This could fundamentally change the way organizations approach risk management and security planning.

3. **Increased demand for AI and data science skills:** As GenAI technologies become more central to cybersecurity operations, there is likely to be a growing demand for professionals with expertise in AI, machine learning, and data science. This may require significant changes in the cybersecurity industry's education, training, and recruitment practices and greater collaboration and cross-pollination with other domains,

7. CONCLUSION

such as computer science, statistics, and cognitive psychology.

4. **Emergence of new business models and service offerings:** The integration of GenAI into cybersecurity could also give rise to new business models and service offerings, such as AI-powered managed security services, predictive threat intelligence platforms, or autonomous incident response systems. This could create new opportunities for innovation and growth in the cybersecurity industry but may also disrupt traditional vendor-customer relationships and competitive dynamics.

5. **Increased complexity and opacity of cybersecurity systems:** As GenAI technologies become more deeply embedded in cybersecurity systems and processes, there is a risk that these systems could become increasingly complex and opaque, making it difficult for humans to understand, trust, and control them. This could create new challenges for accountability, transparency, and oversight in the cybersecurity industry and may require developing new tools, standards, and governance frameworks to ensure the responsible and ethical use of GenAI.

These are just a few examples of the potential long-term impacts of AI-powered cybersecurity on the industry itself. As GenAI technologies continue to evolve and mature, it will be essential for cybersecurity professionals, organizations, and regulators to monitor and adapt to these impacts proactively and work collaboratively to ensure that the benefits of GenAI are realized. At the same time, the risks and challenges will need to be effectively managed.

7.3.2 Broader societal implications and the need for ongoing dialogue

Beyond the cybersecurity industry, adopting GenAI technologies in this domain will likely have significant societal implications. Some of the potential broader societal implications include:

1. Enhanced security and resilience of critical infrastructure: The use of GenAI in cybersecurity could help to enhance the security and resilience of critical infrastructure systems, such as energy grids, transportation networks, and financial systems, which are increasingly vulnerable to cyber-attacks. GenAI could help reduce the risk of catastrophic failures and disruptions in these essential services by enabling more proactive, adaptive, and autonomous approaches to threat detection and response.

2. Protection of individual privacy and civil liberties: The application of GenAI in cybersecurity could also have significant implications for personal privacy and civil rights. On the one hand, GenAI-powered systems could help protect individuals' sensitive data and online activities from malicious actors and cyber threats. On the other hand, the use of GenAI for surveillance, profiling, or other invasive security practices could erode privacy rights and enable new forms of discrimination or manipulation. Ensuring that strong privacy and civil liberties protections guide using GenAI in cybersecurity will be essential to maintain public trust and prevent abuse.

3. Heightened risks of AI-enabled cyber attacks and arms races: As GenAI technologies become more powerful and accessible, there is also a risk that malicious actors could use them to develop new

7. CONCLUSION

and more sophisticated forms of cyber attacks, such as AI-enabled social engineering, autonomous malware, or intelligent botnets. This could lead to a dangerous escalation of cyber threats and an arms race between attackers and defenders, potentially destabilizing national and international security. Developing effective strategies to prevent and mitigate these risks will require close collaboration among governments, industry, and civil society.

4. Impact on the workforce and skills development: The adoption of GenAI in cybersecurity could also have significant implications for the broader workforce and skills development. As certain tasks and roles become automated or augmented by AI, there may be a need for large-scale retraining and upskilling programs to help workers adapt to new job requirements and opportunities. At the same time, the growing demand for AI and data science skills in cybersecurity and other domains may exacerbate existing skills gaps and inequalities, requiring targeted investments in education and workforce development to ensure that the benefits of AI are widely accessible.

5. Ethical and societal implications of AI decision-making: Using GenAI in cybersecurity raises fundamental questions about the ethical and societal impacts of delegating important security decisions to AI systems. As GenAI technologies become more autonomous and influential in shaping cybersecurity practices and policies, there is a risk that they could perpetuate or amplify existing biases, errors, or unintended consequences. Ensuring that the development and deployment of GenAI are guided by strong ethical principles and human oversight will be essential to maintaining accountability and aligning these technologies with broader societal values and priorities.

To navigate these complex societal implications and ensure that the public good guides the adoption of GenAI in cybersecurity, fostering ongoing dialogue and collaboration among diverse stakeholders, including cybersecurity professionals, AI researchers, policymakers, ethicists, and the general public, will be essential. This dialogue should aim to:

- Build shared understanding and awareness of the potential benefits, risks, and challenges of GenAI in cybersecurity and how these may evolve.
- Develop collaborative and inclusive processes for setting priorities, standards, and guidelines for the responsible development and deployment of GenAI in cybersecurity.
- Foster cross-disciplinary research and innovation to address key technical, ethical, and societal challenges, such as ensuring the robustness, transparency, and accountability of GenAI systems.
- Promote public engagement and participation in shaping the future of AI-powered cybersecurity through education, outreach, and deliberative forums.
- Establish ongoing mechanisms for monitoring, assessing, and adapting to the societal impacts of GenAI in cybersecurity and for ensuring that these technologies remain aligned with evolving public values and expectations.

By engaging in this ongoing dialogue and collaboration, we can work towards a future in which the transformative potential of AI-powered cybersecurity is realized in a way that is ethical, responsible, and beneficial for all of society. While the challenges and uncertainties ahead are significant, so are the opportunities to harness the power of GenAI to create a more secure, resilient, and trustworthy digital world.

As we conclude this book, we invite readers to continue exploring and

7. CONCLUSION

engaging with the rapidly evolving landscape of GenAI in cybersecurity and to join us in shaping a future in which these technologies are developed and deployed in service of the greater good. By working together across disciplines, sectors, and communities, we can ensure that the promise of AI-powered cybersecurity is fulfilled while mitigating the risks and challenges that lie ahead. The future of cybersecurity is ours to shape, and the decisions and actions we take today will have profound implications for future generations.

Appendix A. Tools

Threat Detection & Prevention

Commercial:

- CrowdStrike Falcon (EDR platform with AI-powered threat detection)
- Palo Alto Networks Prisma (combines endpoint, network, and cloud security with AI for threat detection)
- MacAfee MVISION EDR (uses AI to analyze endpoint data and identify threats)

Open-Source:

- Security Onion (security monitoring platform with threat detection capabilities) [https://securityonion.org/]
- Suricata (open-source IDS/IPS with threat intelligence feeds) [https://suricata.io/]
- OSSEC (open-source HIDS for log analysis and intrusion detection)

APPENDIX A. TOOLS

Security Operations

Commercial:

- LogRhythm SIEM (security information and event management with AI-powered analytics)
- Demisto SOAR platform (automates security workflows and incident response)
- Darktrace Enterprise Immune System (uses AI for autonomous threat detection and response)

Open-Source:

- ELK Stack (Elasticsearch, Logstash, Kibana) - powerful log analysis platform for security data [https://www.elastic.co/products/elastic-stack]
- Wazuh (open-source SIEM with log analysis, intrusion detection, and vulnerability scanning) [https://wazuh.com/]
- Security Onion (mentioned earlier) also offers SIEM functionalities

Vulnerability Management

Commercial:

- Qualys VM (vulnerability management platform with prioritization and remediation tools) [https://www.qualys.com/]
- Rapid7 InsightVM (identifies, prioritizes, and helps manage vulnerabilities)
- Tenable (offers various vulnerability management solutions with AI-powered scanning) [https://www.tenable.com/]

Open-Source:

- OpenVAS (open-source vulnerability scanner with a large vulnerability database) [https://www.openvas.org/]
- Nessus Professional (free version of a popular vulnerability scanner) [https://www.tenable.com/products/nessus]
- Open Source Security Information Management (OSIM) tools like AlienVault OSSIM can also be used for vulnerability management. [https://www.alienvault.com/products/ossim]

Deception Technology

Commercial:

- Mandiant Red Team Deception
- McAfee Deception Cloud
- Deepwatch Deception Platform

Open-Source:

- Honeypot Project (various tools), https://www.honeynet.org/
- Glastopf (honeypot framework)

Cloud Security Tools

Commercial:

- McAfee Cloud Workload Security
- Palo Alto Networks Prisma Cloud
- CrowdStrike Falcon Cloud Workload Protection

Open-Source:

- CloudSploit (security posture management for cloud infrastructure),https://github.com/aquasecurity/cloudsploit
- Open-Audit (cloud security posture assessment),https://www.open-audit.org/downloads.php
- Cloud-Mapper (cloud infrastructure discovery and mapping) https://github.com/duo-labs/cloudmapper

Identity and Access Management (IAM) Tools

Commercial:

- Microsoft Azure Active Directory with Azure AD Identity Protection
- Okta Advanced Server Access,https://www.okta.com/
- SailPoint IdentityAI

Open-Source:

- OpenIAM (identity and access management framework), https://www.openiam.com/
- Keycloak (open-source identity and access management), https://www.keycloak.org/
- FreeRADIUS (RADIUS server for network access control) https://freeradius.org/

Important Note: While open-source solutions offer advantages in terms of cost and customization, they often require more technical expertise to deploy and maintain compared to commercial offerings with user-friendly interfaces and dedicated support. When choosing between commercial and open-source solutions, it's crucial to consider your organization's security needs, technical capabilities, and budget.

Appendix B. Resources

Websites

- **What is AI in Cybersecurity?** by Sophos: This webpage introduces AI in cybersecurity. It explains what AI is and how it can improve cybersecurity defenses. The webpage also discusses some benefits and challenges of using AI in cybersecurity.
- **AI and Cybersecurity: A New Era by** Morgan Stanley: This report discusses AI's potential to revolutionize cybersecurity. It explores how AI can detect and respond to cyberattacks and prevent them from happening in the first place.
- **AI in cybersecurity: A double-edged sword** by Deloitte: This article discusses the benefits and challenges of using AI in cybersecurity. It highlights that both attackers and defenders can use AI, and it is important to be aware of the risks associated with AI before deploying it in a cybersecurity context.
- **Artificial Intelligence (AI) Cybersecurity by** IBM: This webpage from IBM provides an overview of how AI is used to improve cybersecurity. It discusses how AI can detect threats, prevent attacks, and improve incident response.
- **AI Cybersecurity: 31 Companies to Know** by Built-In: This article lists 31 companies developing AI-powered cybersecurity solutions

and briefly describes each company and its products.

Books

- **Hacking Algorithms: How Malicious Actors Use Machine Learning and Data Science to Attack Systems** by Gregory Tremper: This book discusses how malicious actors use machine learning and data science to attack systems. It gives readers the knowledge and tools to defend against these attacks.
- **Artificial Intelligence for Cyber Warfare: Offense and Defense** by Mikko Russonen: This book explores using artificial intelligence in cyber warfare. It discusses how AI can automate cyberattacks and develop new and more sophisticated attack techniques. The book also discusses how AI can be used to defend against cyberattacks.
- **Machine Learning and Security by** Vigneshwaran Ravi and G. Sekar: This book provides a comprehensive overview of machine learning and its applications in security. It covers various topics, including anomaly detection, intrusion detection, and fraud detection.

Podcasts

- The Malicious Life Podcast is a podcast that covers a wide range of cybersecurity topics, including AI-powered security.
- CyberWire Podcast provides daily news and analysis of cybersecurity threats. In several episodes, it has also covered AI-powered security.
- Security Now is a security expert podcast by Steve Gibson. The podcast covers a wide range of security topics, including AI-powered security.

These are just a few of the many resources available on AI-powered cybersecurity. By learning more about AI and its potential applications in cybersecurity, you can help your organization stay ahead of the curve and protect itself from cyberattacks.

About the Author

Edgardo Fernandez Climent, an accomplished IT leader with over two decades of experience, has significantly contributed to infrastructure, networks, and cybersecurity. His exceptional leadership skills and strategic vision have positioned him as a prominent figure in the industry. After graduating with honors in Computer Information Systems, Edgardo pursued an MBA and a Master's in Management Information Systems, further enhancing his expertise. He also holds several industry certifications, such as PMP, ITIL4, and Security+, demonstrating his commitment to professional development and staying at the forefront of industry standards.

Edgardo has consistently demonstrated his ability to lead organizations through complex technological transformations throughout his career. His deep understanding of emerging technologies and industry trends has enabled him to develop and implement innovative strategies that drive business growth and ensure technological resilience. Edgardo's leadership in navigating the ever-changing landscape of cybersecurity has been instrumental in safeguarding organizations against the evolving threats of the digital world.

As a visionary leader, Edgardo is known for his ability to inspire and motivate teams to achieve excellence. He fosters a culture of continuous learning and encourages his team members to embrace new technologies and develop their skills. Edgardo's commitment to mentoring and developing the next generation of IT leaders has profoundly impacted the industry as he shares his knowledge and experiences to empower others to succeed.

Edgardo's leadership style is characterized by his ability to build strong relationships, promote collaboration, and drive results. He has a proven track record of successfully leading cross-functional teams and aligning IT initiatives with business objectives. His strategic thinking and technical expertise have enabled him to develop and execute transformative initiatives that have delivered significant value to the organizations he has served.

Today, as a highly sought-after consultant in the IT industry, Edgardo continues to be at the forefront of shaping the technological landscape. His leadership and expertise are highly valued by organizations seeking to drive innovation, optimize their IT infrastructure, and strengthen their cybersecurity posture. Edgardo's journey is a testament to the power of visionary leadership, continuous learning, and a relentless pursuit of excellence in the ever-evolving field of information technology.

You can connect with me on:
- https://fernandezcliment.com
- https://twitter.com/efernandezclime
- https://www.facebook.com/edgardo.fernandez.climent
- https://amazon.com/author/efernandezcliment

Subscribe to my newsletter:

✉ https://fernandezcliment.com/join-our-mail-list

Also by Edgardo Fernandez Climent

AIOps: Revolutionizing IT Operations with Artificial Intelligence

"AIOps: Revolutionizing IT Operations with Artificial Intelligence" is a must-read for IT professionals looking to leverage the transformative power of AI and machine learning in IT operations. This comprehensive guide demystifies the concepts, technologies, and best practices behind AIOps, enabling readers to implement intelligent automation, predictive analytics, and data-driven decision-making in their organizations.

The book begins by introducing the fundamental principles and components of AIOps, including data ingestion, anomaly detection, root cause analysis, and automated remediation. It then delves into real-world use cases and applications, showcasing how AIOps can revolutionize incident management, performance optimization, capacity planning, and user experience.

Readers will learn how to build and train AI models, integrate AIOps with existing IT processes and tools, and establish governance frameworks for responsible and ethical AI deployment. The book also explores the organizational and cultural aspects of AIOps adoption, providing strategies for change management, skill development, and continuous improvement.

Through practical examples, case studies, and expert insights, this book empowers IT professionals to harness the full potential of AIOps and drive digital transformation in their organizations. Whether you are an IT manager, system administrator, or data scientist, this book provides the knowledge and guidance needed to succeed in AI-driven IT operations.

AI-Powered Agile: Revolutionizing Project Management with Artificial Intelligence

Discover how the transformative power of artificial intelligence (AI) is revolutionizing agile project management with "AI-Powered Agile: Revolutionizing Project Management with AI." This groundbreaking book explores the intersection of AI and agile, revealing how AI technologies can be leveraged to enhance and optimize every aspect of the agile lifecycle.

In this book, you'll learn how to:

- Harness AI-powered insights and recommendations to streamline sprint planning and backlog management

- Utilize AI-driven virtual assistants and sentiment analysis to optimize team collaboration and communication

- Implement adaptive project management practices using machine learning and predictive analytics

- Mitigate risks and improve decision-making with AI-powered forecasting and scenario planning

- Foster a culture of continuous learning and experimentation with AI in agile teams

The author provides a comprehensive framework for integrating AI into agile practices through in-depth research, real-world case studies, and practical insights. They address critical challenges and considerations, such as data quality, ethical implications, and cultural adoption, ensuring that you have a holistic understanding of AI's impact on agile project management.

Whether you are an agile practitioner, project manager, or business leader, "AI-powered Agile" equips you with the knowledge and tools to leverage AI's power in your agile projects. The book offers a compelling vision of how humans and artificial intelligence can work together to achieve exceptional results and drive organizational success.

Key features of the book include:

- Comprehensive coverage of AI technologies and their applications in agile project management
- Practical templates and tools for implementing AI-powered agile practices
- Real-world case studies and examples from industry leaders
- Strategies for overcoming challenges and fostering a culture of AI adoption
- Future trends and opportunities for AI in agile project management

"AI-Powered Agile" is not just a book but a roadmap for navigating the future of project management in an increasingly AI-driven world. It is an essential guide for anyone looking to stay ahead of the curve and unlock the full potential of AI in their agile practices.

Take advantage of this transformative journey that will reshape how you think about and execute agile project management in the age of AI. Get your copy of "AI-Powered Agile: Revolutionizing Project Management with Artificial Intelligence" today!

Leveraging Generative AI in IT Project Management: A Practical Guide

"Leveraging Generative AI in IT Project Management: A Practical Guide" is an indispensable resource for IT project managers and professionals seeking to navigate the complexities of modern project landscapes with the innovative power of Generative AI (GenAI). This comprehensive guide begins with a foundational preface on GenAI's significance in IT project management and offers readers an instructive roadmap on utilizing the book to its full potential. This book covers all the essential grounds, from the fundamentals of GenAI technologies, key concepts, and their application in IT projects to the strategic integration of GenAI for project planning, documentation, and risk management.

Through detailed chapters, readers will learn how to set up their projects for success with GenAI, including choosing the right models, integrating AI into existing systems, and using GenAI for dynamic documentation and real-time project tracking. The book also delves into the softer aspects of project management, such as fostering an AI-ready culture, managing human-AI collaboration, and navigating the governance and ethical challenges AI technologies pose. With a focus on practical applications, each chapter is enriched with case studies, examples, and best practices for leveraging GenAI to enhance team collaboration, optimize resource allocation, and make strategic decisions.

Addressing future trends and innovations, the book prepares project managers for the evolving IT project management landscape, emphasizing the importance of sustainable and ethical AI development. The guide concludes with an epilogue that reflects on the paradigm shifts in project management and the enduring role of human ingenuity in an AI-driven world. Complemented by appendices offering a glossary of terms, resources for further learning, and a directory of software and tools, this guide is a must-have for anyone looking to leverage GenAI to drive project success in the digital age.

The S.M.A.R.T. Advantage: Achieve Your Goals with Precision Using Google Gemini

Master Your Goals in the Digital Age – The S.M.A.R.T. Advantage, Amplified by Google Gemini

Ditch endless scrolling and transform your goals into reality with this revolutionary guide. Elevate the classic S.M.A.R.T. framework using Google Gemini's cutting-edge insights for laser-focused action plans, data-driven strategies, and unstoppable adaptability.

This book empowers you to:

Gain laser-focus with precision research, transforming vague dreams into actionable steps.

Set realistic timelines, anticipate challenges, and track meaningful progress.

Align goals with your core values and uncover hidden opportunities.

Stop wishing for change – start achieving it! Harness the power of Google Gemini and become the unstoppable architect of your success.

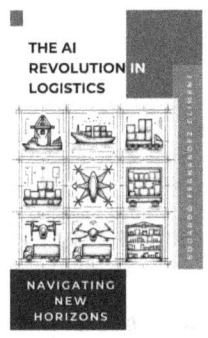

The AI Revolution in Logistics: Navigating New Horizons

Discover the transformative power of artificial intelligence (AI) in logistics with "The AI Revolution in Logistics: Navigating New Horizons." This comprehensive guide explores the latest advancements, use cases, and best practices for leveraging AI to optimize and revolutionize logistics operations.

As the logistics industry faces increasing complexity, customer expectations, and global competition, AI has emerged as a game-changing technology that can drive unprecedented efficiency, agility, and innovation. From demand forecasting and inventory optimization to autonomous vehicles and robotic warehouses, AI is reshaping every aspect of the logistics landscape.

In this book, you'll learn how to harness the power of AI to streamline your logistics processes, reduce costs, improve customer service, and gain a competitive edge. Key topics covered include:

The evolution of AI in logistics and its transformative potential

Key AI technologies and their applications in logistics, such as machine learning, natural language processing, computer vision, and robotics

Real-world case studies and success stories from industry leaders

Practical strategies for implementing AI in logistics, including data management, talent development, and change management

Ethical and responsible AI practices in logistics, including data privacy, algorithmic fairness, and human-machine collaboration

The future of AI-powered logistics, including emerging trends, challenges, and opportunities

Whether you're a logistics professional, supply chain executive, or technology enthusiast, "The AI Revolution in Logistics" provides the insights, tools, and guidance you need to navigate the AI-driven future of logistics. With expert insights, real-world examples, and actionable advice, this book is an essential resource for anyone looking to unlock the full potential of AI in logistics and stay ahead of the curve in this rapidly evolving industry.

Take advantage of the AI revolution in logistics. Order your copy of "The AI Revolution in Logistics: Navigating New Horizons" today and start your journey towards more innovative, faster, and more efficient logistics operations.

www.ingramcontent.com/pod-product-compliance
Lightning Source LLC
Chambersburg PA
CBHW050056230526
45470CB00004B/1548